## DEDICATION

Dedicated to the Holy Spirit, my constant
Companion, Comforter, and Guide;
and to the many who continue to
allow You to lead us through life's
daily adventures and challenges.

The Rock of Roseville
725 Vernon St., Roseville, CA
95678 U.S.A.

ISBN # 978-1-943157-34-1

# IT'S A SUPERNATURAL LIFE!

*Finding God In Your
Failures, Fears, and Successes*

# FRANCIS ANFUSO

# ACKNOWLEDGMENTS

As this book is a recounting of divine appointments I never authored and many others helped facilitate, I have to mention their involvement in birthing this testimonial.

It all begins with my Heavenly Father, who continues to teach me what real fathers are like. Then there's Jesus, the Lover of my soul, and my Rescuer. I tear up just thinking about Him. I was so lost, so stupid, so selfish...I think you get my drift. But, He is so safe, so selfless, such a Savior...my Hero! And last, but never least, the Holy Spirit, my great Comforter and Guide into all truth and truly living.

Next up would be my Mother. I am finishing writing this section on Mother's Day 2016, another reminder that her timeless prayers are still at work. The only prayer partner she ever had was Jesus, and yet, they met the minimum quorum of "if two or three are gathered in my name, there am I among them." We, her children, know the power of her appeals.

Taking over for my mother was my beautiful wife Suzie, more stable than most, the best wife, mother and friend I have ever known. She continues to be the keel in the hull of my life, helping me remain stable, safe, and sane, which is no small task.

My anointed daughters, Deborah and Havilah, continue to be a sign and a wonder. Now married to marvelous men, Daniel and Ben, they and their magnificent children, Judah, Gabriella, Hudson, William, Wesley, Grayson and Beckham, remind me daily that generations are watching my life and counting on me to live and finish well. May each of them, one day, read this daily devotional and be inspired to be led by God's Spirit as well.

Then there are my intercessors and co-laborers. My intercessory team leader: Adena Hodges; armor bearer: Gary DeGennaro; personal assistant for many years: Lydia Birks; additional intercessors, elders, friends, congregation members, regional leaders, etc., all perfectly positioned by God to pray, help, and bless my life beyond words.

For many years now, my books and messages have been written with an angelic choir singing in my headphones: the worship leaders from IHOPKC, the International House of Prayer in Kansas City. Their anointed worship has provided an atmosphere of peace and abandonment that is the perfect soil for every seed-word I write. In particular, the Worship With The Word sets led by Laura Hackett Park. Thank you!

Lastly, the practitioners who refined this book into a finished product; chief editor: Kaycie Simmons Edeh, proofreaders: Lydia Birks and Judy McCollough, and graphics and layout: Hans "No Problem" Bennewitz.

Eternal thanks to each of you!

# INTRODUCTION

My wife and I lived in South Lake Tahoe for nine years. We would often drive from the top of this mountain lake down into the Sacramento Valley. At times, on the downgrade, I would pick up speed. Once, as I was cruising along, I heard this loud voice say, "Stay in your own lane and drive 55!" It wasn't God. It was a Highway Patrolman on his loud speaker. That expression became a part of my wife and my driving dialogue. Whenever I would drive too fast or "braille drive," as she calls it when I linger over the protruding lane dividers, she would say, "Stay in your own lane and drive 55!" It became a tongue-in-cheek comment that always brought a smile.

Ironically, while writing this book, God showed me that this memorable statement we have probably repeated a hundred times, really defines much of my Christian life, though it took me 30 years to realize its prophetic significance.

In my insecurity, I have at times wondered why I had such an odd personality, calling, and way of ministering. Yet, I had my own lane. Secondly, my twin brother was the guy growing up who went across lanes at 90 miles an hour. I was the more conservative twin, even though this might surprise some people.

Once, after ministering in a large and wealthy church in Dallas, Texas, the pastor said after the service, "You have the most conservative ministry in the Gifts of the Spirit." I know he may not have considered his assessment a compliment, but I did. I wanted to live on the edge, but not over the edge; to do exploits, but not be exploited by impulses or deception. Decades of being a whole-hearted disciple of Jesus, and having done enough autopsies on fallen spiritual leaders, merely affirmed this safe perspective.

Another way of saying this was expressed by Lance Hahn, a young evangelical pastor, at our first of many luncheons. "You are the sanest person in the crazy wing!" We laughed, but I loved it. I wanted to turn over tables, rub spit in blind men's eyes, and empty hospitals, but ONLY if my heavenly Father was directing me to do so. This brand of being conservatively crazy has made my following Jesus a great adventure, but not a distracting disaster.

Nevertheless, crazy experiences have been my norm! Suzie and I lived on a golf course for a few years, where we were able to take wonderful prayer and fellowship walks together. One day we found a 9-iron on one of the greens and so walked on to the next few holes to see if we might find whom it belonged to. We passed a couple of groups and finally arrived at the 16th hole, adjacent to our home.

To our surprise, a highly respected senior pastor in our region was on the tee box about to hit. His name was Dr. Glen Cole, renowned as a patriarch in the Sacramento region and a national leader within the Assemblies of God. Though it wasn't his golf club, he agreed to turn it in at the clubhouse. We had a wonderful exchange!

But that was a strange encounter, to say the least!

As you will soon realize in reading these devotionals, I believe, as the Bible says, "It is God who is working in me, both to will and to do of His good pleasure.†" Why is something happening? God is wanting to show me something. What was His purpose in allowing me to meet a major regional giant on my home hole? And instead of him symbolically giving me something, I gave something to him.

I spent a few years prayerfully pondering this, especially after he went to be with Jesus a short time later. What could I possibly give him that he would value? I finally came to this conclusion: during the last few years of his life he would regularly attend our City Pastor's Fellowship meetings, not to lead but to support. He made me nervous whenever I spoke there, because of his stature, but he was always extremely gracious. He cared! He cared about our city! He cared about the next generation of leaders being raised up! And as the success of these meetings became apparent, we had no bigger cheerleader than Glen Cole.

I now believe we were fulfilling a lifelong dream of this anointed father: the Body of Christ is coming together. Unity is not a pipe dream, but an ever-increasing reality. To me, the 9-iron represented the fruit and gifts of the Holy Spirit that this godly saint so loved. All that we do now continues to make his dream a reality.

So, in recounting some of the miraculous divine interventions during my life, I have tried to let God be the initiator, and not myself. Since He is the author and finisher, He gets every speck of glory. Jesus, assessing our abilities, was not overstating His point when He said, "...apart from me you can do nothing." Without Him, we can do nothing of eternal value... and nothing that truly transforms other people's lives. He alone is the Master Scriptwriter. My only shot at living a blessed and fruitful life is being an obedient script-doer. "Jesus, make it so, for I long to do Your will alone!"

I have signed every email for many years with a delightful quote from the great pioneer missionary to China, Hudson Taylor, "First it is impossible. Then it is difficult. Then it is done." My failures didn't sabotage me, my fears didn't keep me from believing for the impossible, and my successes were mere manifestations of the incredible grace of God.

**Francis Anfuso**
October 2016

† PHILIPPIANS 2:13, NKJV

## The B.C. Years (1949–1972)

## The Early Years (1972–1975)

## The Evangelistic Years (1976–1984)

## The Pastoral Years (2000–2008)

## The Sacramento Years (2009–2013)

## The Intercessory Years (2013 & BEYOND)

# THE B.C
## YEARS

*1949—1972*

# THE B.C
YEARS

MY DAD & ME

HE REMEMBERED MY 13TH BIRTHDAY

MY FIRST HOLY COMMUNION

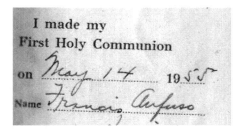

MY FATHER, THE POLITICIAN

JOSEPH LIVING IN INDIA & NEPAL

HIPPIES: BRUCE, JOSEPH & FRANCIS

POLITICAL DINNER FOR VICE PRESIDENT

DAD BEING KNIGHTED BY THE POPE

PRESIDENT KENNEDY & VICE PRESIDENT JOHNSON

# MY FATHER'S BLESSING CHANGED MY LIFE

**PRINCIPLE:** MY FATHER HAD A CLEARER VIEW OF WHO I WAS THAN I EVER THOUGHT POSSIBLE.

My father was a famous political figure who was even knighted by the Pope; but as a child, he abandoned me. Consequently, on the day he died of a heart attack, there was no one I hated more than him. It grieves me to write this, but it's true.

**Ironically, now 50 years after his death, no person's words encourage me more!**

I am only aware of one sentence my father wrote about his impressions of me as a young boy. It was handwritten on a picture of him with the Pope, and it read, "To my son Frank, whose benevolence will ingratiate the hearts of many." Big words for a little boy, but once I understood their meaning, they have blessed me more than anything anyone has ever said about me. He saw me! I had value! My father's blessing branded my life!

We each grow up searching for perfect love. Yet God alone is the Father we've always wanted; the perfect parent we each long for. Many times, when our earthly parents miss the mark of God's selfless love, a wound is created. Your dad may have overlooked you, but God never forgot you. Your mom may not have given you emotional support, but Jesus wants to undergird your life with His love and care.

The Bible says, "Even if my father and mother abandon me, the Lord will hold me close."[1] My Father in Heaven never abandoned me, not even when I was openly denying Him.

**God knows what we're looking for—what we're longing for. We want Him! And the best news we'll ever hear is... He wants us too!**

**SCRIPTURE** *"Then Jacob called his sons and said, 'Gather yourselves together, that I may tell you what shall happen to you in days to come.'" (Genesis 49:1)*

1. PSALMS 27:10, NLT

# AN ABANDONED & REJECTED CHILDHOOD

**PRINCIPLE:** GOD CAN MAKE A WONDERFUL LIFE OUT OF AN IMPOSSIBLE CHILDHOOD.

When my mother became pregnant with my twin brother Joseph and me, my father wanted her to have an abortion. He already had three older children. As my mother told the story, "I went to a doctor, got some pills, came home, and he told me to take them." It's a painful description of how much my father didn't want more children but true nonetheless.

We were born in 1949. He was elected to the U.S. Congress in 1950.

Joseph and I would spend seven years of our childhood, from 11 to 17 years old, living in an oppressive boarding school. We could never talk in classrooms, hallways, or dormitories. They closed the boarding school down the year we graduated. We never again saw any of the kids we went to school with. I try not to think about my time there.

Desperate for love and affection I would periodically get up before the other boys and go to a religious service in a language I couldn't understand, to worship a God I didn't believe in. To indicate I wanted to be awakened, I would have to tie a towel at the end of my bed. The man in charge would then know to shake me to get up. It was those precious moments of touch, even by the hand of someone I significantly disliked, that made it all worth it.

**I had been touched! Not in anger or correction, but I imagined because someone cared. We live in a world desperate for a touch of kindness, from a caring hand, with no other motive than unconditional love.**

I realize when I hug people, it may be the only hug they get that day, or even that week.

Who in your life desperately needs a touch of kindness?

**SCRIPTURE** *"When my father and my mother forsake me, then the Lord will take care of me." (Psalm 27:10 NKJV) (Matthew 8:3, 17:7, Isaiah 53:5)*

# RIDDLE BEHIND THE ORIGINAL SEVEN ASTRONAUTS

**PRINCIPLE:** BLESSINGS FROM OUR PARENTS MAY REVEAL HIDDEN TREASURE.

My father was on the House of Representatives' Committee on Science and Astronautics. In 1962, he attended a dinner at the Waldorf Astoria in New York City, honoring the original Mercury Seven American astronauts: Scott Carpenter, Gordon Cooper, John Glenn, Gus Grissom, Wally Schirra, Alan Shepard, and Deke Slayton. For some reason my father had each of them sign the dinner menu and address it to me saying, "Frank, we hope you will become one of us!" It was a gesture I questioned for decades. Since I had never met his lofty expectations for me, I filed it away as another request I could not fulfill. **For decades it served as a reminder of what I would never be, not what I could be.**

I now believe I was terribly wrong!

In 2015, I examined the date on the menu and realized the dinner was six days after my 13th birthday. My father, who rarely saw me, was sending me a birthday wish. It seems so obvious now, but it was a hidden riddle until I was sufficiently healed of my father wounds.

In March, 2017, the Holy Spirit showed me the effort it took my father to get those signatures. He had to approach each astronaut individually and say something like this, "I have a son who just had his 13th birthday..." Like Naaman the Syrian general, my father was a leper to me, but he was willing to dip in that Jordan River seven times. My father did see me.

As incomprehensible as my pain once was, so now is the joy of a healed heart. **Once a prisoner of tormenting memories and a desperate longing for a dad, my relationship with my Heavenly Father now provides all of the time and attention I need—showering me with every imaginable gift a son could want.**

Now, many years after the battle for my childhood heart was fought, I find my-self carefully examining the remains of past emotions—the relics of relational ruins. At times, all I seem to uncover are the dead remnants of an irreplaceable past. **But at other more hopeful moments, my efforts cause unparalleled revelations to surface that I will treasure for eternity.**

**SCRIPTURE** *"And he will turn the hearts of the fathers to the children, and the hearts of the children to their fathers..." (Malachi 4:6)*

## SUZIE'S RELATIONSHIP WITH HER DAD

1964

**PRINCIPLE:** OUR CONCEPT OF GOD IS PERHAPS MOST AFFECTED BY OUR VIEW OF OUR PARENTS.

When my beautiful wife Suzie was seven years old, a ranch worker tried to touch her inappropriately. Running home to tell her dad, he immediately jumped in his pickup, went down to the barn, and without hesitation fired the man, telling him to, "Get off the property and never come back!" The magnitude of that decision meant that her dad's workload just doubled. Decades later, Suzie realized the power of what her father had done, and told me what impacts her most now is that her dad believed her, without question.

At 20 years old, Suzie was arrested for carrying marijuana across the Canadian border and spent a sleepless night in a felony cell. Suzie thought her parents, with whom she was very close, wouldn't hear about it. But, being a community leader, her dad did. Not knowing he had, she phoned home a week later. Her dad, responding to her call, said, "I heard about the problem you had in Canada."

Suzie was stunned! She held her breath, wondering what would follow. Her dad quickly added, "But that's water under the bridge, Honey. I just want to know how you are!"

**Is it any wonder my wife called her father "Daddy" every day of his life?**

When I married Suzie, even though I had tremendous father wounds in my own life, I made a conscious decision to call him dad. Because of the way he loved Suzie, I knew he was safe enough to merit that title. When he was dying of cancer, I carried him into our home with both of us crying and me saying, "It's OK, Dad!"

**Is there anything more special than a safe father?**

---

**SCRIPTURE** *"...the glory of children is their fathers." (Proverbs 17:6)*

# GOD SPARED MY LIFE MULTIPLE TIMES

**PRINCIPLE:** MORE TIMES THAN WE WILL EVER KNOW ON EARTH, GOD HAS PROTECTED US.

When I was 19 years old, I went to a football game with my twin brother, Joseph, between Rutgers and Princeton. It was a rivalry that had begun in 1883, at the very first college football game ever played. Since Joseph attended Rutgers, when his team won I was elated. Sadly, though, I was also drunk and completely out of control. Shimmying up a goalpost, I had the top of the 32-foot pole under my stomach as hundreds of people below began to tear it down. Much to my dismay, it began to sway perilously back and forth. Even in my diminished state of mind, I knew I was in grave danger, and so held on in sheer terror.

Suddenly, the heavy metal pole snapped. As I continued to hold on, the pole began to fall to the ground. Suddenly, it stopped just four feet from the ground and violently shook me off. With the wind knocked out of me, and looking up from the ground dazed, a stranger walked up and asked if I was OK.

While still gasping for air, I said, "Yes!"

He quickly added, with a stern look on his face, "You're an idiot!"

It was a defining moment in my life!

Until then, I didn't know who I was.

Now, at last I had clarity. I was an idiot!

This humorous image didn't describe all of me, but at that time, it was a partial view. **How many of us wake up eager to climb the imaginary goalposts of shallow recognition, not realizing we'll soon fall?** I may have bowed to foolishness then, but I don't want that to be my legacy.

**My Creator best defines who I am. I will gaze into His eyes to see my true reflection.**

---

**SCRIPTURE** *"Our God is the God of salvation; and to GOD the Lord belong escapes from death." (Psalm 68:20, NKJV)*

# SUICIDAL...EVERY DAY FOR SIX MONTHS

**PRINCIPLE:** WE MUST COME TO THE END OF OUR FALSE SELF BEFORE WE CAN FIND OUR TRUE SELF.

An abortion with my college girlfriend signaled the downfall of our connection. As the relationship declined, so too did my fragile mental state. It seemed my every thought turned to suicide. I would spend days lying in bed, staring at the wall, overcome with self-pity, hating my life, and absolutely unable to dig my way out of my mental quagmire.

I was increasingly unstable.

At the conclusion of college, my friends and I traveled across the country in a packed hippie van, intent on starting a commune in Mexico, but nothing I tried could keep my life from unraveling. Though we still traveled together, by that time, the relationship with my girlfriend was completely over.

After being rejected by authorities at the Mexican border, our motley crew settled for the night on a remote Arizona road. In a deranged state of mind, I wandered aimlessly into the barren desert. Miserable and longing to die on that star-filled night, I took out a pocketknife and began to carve on my wrists. Fortunately, the knife was dull, and my mother's incessant prayers were sharp enough to pierce through the arrogance of my disillusioned heart.

**Kneeling amongst the sagebrush, I screamed to the God I didn't believe in, "God help me!"** Looking back on that fateful moment, there was so much deception in my life I didn't even realize what I had said until many months later. **But the prayer had been prayed, and the God who sees and hears all, responded to my cry.**

---

**SCRIPTURE** *"The steadfast love of the LORD never ceases; his mercies never come to an end..." (Lamentations 3:22) "He also brought me up out of a horrible pit, out of the miry clay, and set my feet upon a rock, and established my steps." (Psalm 40:2)*

**PRINCIPLE:** AT OUR LOWEST MOMENTS, JESUS IS THE ONLY PERSON WE CAN TURN TO FOR HELP.

My life unraveled in one suicidal night, November 14, 1971, in Marysville, California. The hippie van Magical Mystery Tour was over! The Peace, Love Dove Express crashed and burned! I was now threatening suicide constantly. My twin-brother, ex-girlfriend, and best friend didn't know what to do with me. I don't blame them. I didn't know what to do with me.

(I would calculate, years later that on this fateful suicidal night, five miles away, my wife-to-be, Suzie, was being baptized in water and in the Spirit. It would be six months to the day until I would surrender my heart to Jesus as well.)

The next morning, the woman I had given $100 to vacuum away our child in New York City two months before, now gave me $100 to get on a plane and fly away from her life. As the flight took off from Sacramento, California, and my eyes filled with tears, I resolved to either meet God or die. I was going to a place I'd never been, Honolulu, Hawaii, to live in an abandoned parachute on a beach with six lonely people who never said one word to each other. I slept in a mummy sleeping bag suitable for 10 below zero, and I spent every night intermittently sweating and letting mosquitoes eat me.

It was filet-of-my-soul!

But God was at work, and my arrogant rejection of Him would morph into a desperate clinging to my only hope.

**Focusing on my problems had merely lulled me to sleep.**

**Feasting on God's promises would one day awaken me to the life of my dreams.**

SCRIPTURE *"By faith Abraham obeyed when he was called to go out to a place that he was to receive as an inheritance. And he went out, not knowing where he was going." (Hebrews 11:8)*

# DECEPTION REACHED FOR ME AT EVERY TURN

**PRINCIPLE:** GOOD AND EVIL ARE FIGHTING FOR YOUR SOUL AND ETERNAL DESTINY.

Before I received Jesus, the enemy tried to destroy me on many occasions. Once, I almost jumped off a Canadian Rocky Mountain cliff while on a hallucinogenic; the massive rapids far below looked like marshmallows. I was only spared because the woman with me grabbed my arm and said, "What are you doing?"

There was one time during our hippie phase, when four women, with shaved heads standing in a food stamp line, showed us in the Bible that the Beast was going to come out of the Bottomless Pit. They claimed it would happen on New Year's Eve 1971, in Haleakala Crater on the Island of Maui, and that simultaneously, Venusians would rescue us. On that full moon, ten friends and I spent the night waiting, while on drugs. Those four women would later die together following a false prophet.

While travelling with a woman who claimed to come from the planet Venus, she and I walked by a complete stranger who, without breaking stride, briefly glanced at her and said matter-of-factly, "Oh, a Venusian!" I was about to travel with her to South America and would have been in grave danger. She had previously smuggled a large quantity of cocaine from Columbia.

But I received Jesus, and I called off the trip.

Lastly, within a 30-minute timeframe, on the eve of my leaving Maui, I had three physical attacks: a car swerved off the road to hit me while passengers cursed me, a wild dog attacked me, and I just missed being bit by a large poisonous insect. Why all of this? **The enemy knew that the next day I was going to fly to see a close friend who had recently been born again. I too would receive Jesus two days later. Deceptive seductions and attacks are indications of our importance to God.**

**SCRIPTURE** *"The steadfast love of the LORD never ceases; his mercies never come to an end..." (Lamentations 3:22)*

# BROKEN HEARTED FROM A BROKEN RELATIONSHIP

1971

**PRINCIPLE:** GOD ALONE CAN COMFORT AND HEAL OUR BROKEN HEARTS.

I fell in love with a girl in college before she knew I existed. She was the campus beauty queen, and my heart was so infatuated I actually went to school in England for a semester just to get away from seeing her. When I returned, I even made an appointment to meet with her and share my emotional journey. She was polite and kind, and I felt a little better that my obsession with her was at least in the open.

Ironically, a short time later, we lived together for a year and a half. When she became pregnant and begged me to get married and have the child, I told her I didn't believe in marriage and didn't want children. It was the deathblow to our relationship! Even though I had strong feelings for her, my selfishness won out. This led to six months of battling suicidal thoughts, ultimately ending in me finding my true love, the Lord Jesus Christ.

We are each offered daily opportunities by God to be healed of wounds. Though the process will certainly be painful, it is well worth the struggle. Yet, there are no shortcuts, only detours of denial. And, **unless we allow God to heal us, we will remain stuck in cycles of grief, masking our pain. Battling confusion, shame and anger, we will fight isolation and even depression. Only God can break this discouraging cycle and bring about the resolution and healing we each so desperately need.** If we allow Him, He will help us work through the pain, bringing us to a safe place of healing and hope. As the prophet Jeremiah wrote, "Heal me, O Lord, and I shall be healed; save me, and I shall be saved, for you are my praise."[2]

---

**SCRIPTURE** *"...if the Son sets you free, you will be free indeed..." (John 8:36, NIV)*

2. JEREMIAH 17:14

# BEING SINCERE IS NOT ENOUGH

1971

**PRINCIPLE:** HISTORY IS FILLED WITH SINCERE PEOPLE WHO WERE SINCERELY WRONG.

One of the most common deceptive statements is, "As long as you're sincere, it doesn't make any difference what you believe." As if reality bends to our perceptions. At one time or another, all of us have been "sincerely wrong."

Within a couple of months of arriving on Maui, I was reunited for a short time with my friend Bruce, who, like me, was a sincere seeker and student of other religions. At one point, we knelt together on a remote beach on the Hawaiian Island of Molokai and earnestly prayed, "Jesus, Krishna, Buddha, we can see from reading your teachings that you are not the same person. Would you please reveal yourself to us?"

A short while later Bruce left Hawaii, but was determined to find God. Going into a remote wooded area, his search for the divine led to endlessly chanting prayers to Krishna every day for a full month. Instead of reaching enlightenment, however, his efforts only brought him close to a nervous breakdown.

Returning in desperation to his hometown of Marysville, Bruce walked into the Episcopal Church he had grown up in. It was mid-day and no one was around. Barefoot and wearing a saffron robe, he went to the front of the sanctuary where he knelt before a statue of Jesus hanging on a cross. Collapsing in an emotional heap, he prayed an anguished, sobbing prayer, "I don't know much about You, except what I heard here as a young boy growing up. But, if You can, please help me." **At that moment, Bruce was knocked backward. All of the pressures plaguing his troubled mind were instantly lifted. Every question he had was either answered or suddenly seemed insignificant. He knew God had answered his quest for purpose.**

What deception have you sincerely believed?

**SCRIPTURE** *"Do not be conformed to this world, but be transformed by the renewal of your mind, that by testing you may discern what is the will of God, what is good and acceptable and perfect." (Romans 12:2)*

# "GOD, IF YOU'RE REAL!" HOLE-IN-ONE

**PRINCIPLE:** GOD WILL ALWAYS REVEAL HIMSELF TO A GENUINELY SINCERE, SEEKING PERSON.

My older brother Victor had an encounter with God that was a direct answer to prayer. He was a very successful, Madison Avenue lawyer in New York City. One day in February of 1972, while playing golf in Palm Beach, Florida, he began to complain to God, "I've been reading the Bible and trying to find you for two years, are you really there?"

At that moment, Vic said, "I felt like something took over me. The next four holes I had all pars. It seemed like a movie! The fifth hole was a 211-yard, par three, with a raised green. I hit the ball and knew it went on the green but couldn't find it. So, I dropped a new ball and putted it in the hole. When I pulled the pin, two balls came out. **Shocked, I shouted, 'Ok, You're really there! Stop! I can't take it anymore!' The fear of the Lord had come upon me.**"

It took my brother another 17 months before he would surrender his life to Jesus, but a seed had been planted that would eventually change his life.

Have you asked God to reveal Himself to you?

He promises, "You will seek me and find me, when you seek me with all your heart."[3]

**God's not a God of can't and don't. He's a God of can and do.**

**He's not trying to rain on your party. He wants to invite you to His!**

---

**SCRIPTURE** *"In my distress I called to the LORD, and he answered me." (Psalm 120:1)*

---

3. JEREMIAH 29:13

# THE EARLY

*1972–1975* YEARS

# THE EARLY
_1972–1975_ YEARS

THE SMARTSVILLE REVIVAL—1973

OUR JESUS FREAK TRUCK W/ #1 DOCTRINE

## Ministers' Arrested At High School

Three Marysville men listing their occupations as ministers were arrested by Marysville police yesterday at Marysville High School on charges of disrupting school activities.

Charles Bruce Kimmel, 26, and Francis Salvador Anfuso, 24, both of 700 I St., and John Richey Moe, 29, of 1013 Harris St., were booked in the Marysville City jail about 12:30 p.m. yesterday.

MISTAKES HAVE CONSEQUENCES

PREACHING DURING THE SMARTSVILLE REVIVAL

SHARING THE GOSPEL WITH 10,000 PEOPLE AT OUR LOCAL FOOTBALL GAME

SUZIE'S PARENTS AND MY MOTHER

MARRIAGE FOUNDED ON GOD'S WORD

SINGING "SUZIE, I WON'T FAIL YOU" ON OUR WEDDING DAY

# DAY 12 HITCHHIKING "FREAK" ON MAUI

**PRINCIPLE:** AT TIMES, THE PEOPLE WHO IMPACT US THE MOST WILL LOOK NOTHING LIKE US.

When I lived on the Hawaiian Island of Maui, I was picked up hitchhiking by a pastor, in an immaculate VW Van, with two very conservative looking young women. It was beyond odd! I was a longhaired, hippie "freak" (a term we used to affirm our counter-culture identity). He was so kind, even inviting me to a wedding. I left the ride very grateful but completely mystified as to why he treated me with such respect.

Years later, when I developed an evangelistic training course on sharing Christ, he contacted our ministry, and I connected the dots that Pastor Larry Elias was the unusually gracious man who touched my life. We have met on many occasions since then, and I've even spoken in his church.

**The impact of a simple act of obedience goes far beyond what we can see.**

An ex-boxer, named Mordecai Ham, was radically saved. In time, he bought a tent and began to hold evangelistic meetings across the South. On one occasion, when he went into a city, the churches didn't want him there; so he took his tent right outside the city limits.

One night, a teenage boy came to a meeting and got saved. His name was Billy Graham. WOW! A little-known evangelist, who was rejected by fellow Christians but didn't give up, continued to preach the gospel and Billy Graham got saved.

Sounds like **we shouldn't give up when we're doing God's will, because we never know who's on the other side of our obedience. "If you are willing and obedient, you shall eat the good of the land..."[4]**

**SCRIPTURE** *"Why do you call me 'Lord, Lord,' and not do what I tell you?" (Luke 6:46)*

4. ISAIAH 1:19

# DAY 13 CRAZY CAR RIDE ON THE DAY I RECEIVED JESUS

**PRINCIPLE:** GOD WAS WORKING IN OUR LIVES LONG BEFORE WE REALIZED IT.

On the morning of the evening I would receive Jesus as my Lord and Savior, I was hitchhiking after spending the night sleeping on a river. I had gotten back from living in Maui a couple of days before and had been trying to find my twin brother who had sent me a postcard saying he was camped out on the Yuba River near Nevada City. (I would be baptized in that same river a month later.)

I was a full-blown hippie freak and was picked up by a redneck in a truck. I spent the next 25-minutes telling him that he needed God, even though, at that moment, I wouldn't have known God if I tripped over Him. About half way to my destination, there was the Smartsville turnoff. It was there we stopped to pick up another hitchhiker. He got into the truck with a pocket New Testament in his hand. He had just left the Sunday morning service at the Smartsville Community Church where, though I didn't know it, I would come back to receive Jesus later that night. He didn't know the Lord yet either, and had left in the middle of a service, but we both began to tag-team our driver, preaching to him about God for the next 25 minutes.

I never saw the driver again, but four years later I ran into the 2nd hitchhiker. He had become a Christian and was then the principal of a small Christian School. We rejoiced together about all God had done in our lives!

**Have you looked back and seen the footprints of God in your life? He was working on you long before you realized it. But, in retrospect, reflecting and appreciating what He did will provide milestones of memories.**

"...for it is God who works in you, both to will and to work for his good pleasure."[5]

---

**SCRIPTURE** *"Then Elisha prayed and said, 'O Lord, please open his eyes that he may see.' So the Lord opened the eyes of the young man, and he saw..." (2Kings 6:17)*

5. PHILIPPIANS 2:13

# DELIVERED FROM DEMONS

**PRINCIPLE:** THE COUNTERFEIT SUPERNATURAL CAN NEVER COMPETE WITH THE GENUINE.

**When I received Jesus, in 1972, I had a bizarre experience.** During the previous season of my life in Hawaii, I had spent many hours chanting to the Hindu god, Krishna. This opened me up to the supernatural, metaphysical realm, and allowed demonic spiritual entities to attach themselves to my soul and spirit.

In a small country church in Smartsville, California, **I prayed, "Jesus, I don't know if you are who this man says you are, but if you are, do for me what you did for him."** Immediately, the two necklaces I was wearing choked me. One was Japa Beads, used to chant to Krishna, and the other a turquoise necklace, which I believed communicated to Venusians (people from Venus: I will explain more about this later).

Unable to breathe or move my hands to help, I prayed a second prayer, "Jesus, help me!" Instantly, my hands ripped the necklaces off. Hundreds of beads scattered all over the floor, and I could breathe again.

**In that moment, something truly supernatural took place.** After crying for some time, people explained that Jesus Christ, the one true God, had kicked the false gods I had previously worshipped (actually demons) out of my life. I had been born again! It was Mother's Day, May 14. 1972. From the very beginning, I knew it was because of my mother's prayers.

For the next month, I was so high on God I thought I'd never come down. Eventually, I learned my relationship with God was intended to be a walk in faith not feelings.

**So I put my faith in the facts, the Word of God, realizing my feelings would come and go but they are never meant to be my guide.**

SCRIPTURE *"...the working of Satan, with all power, signs, and lying wonders..."* *(2Thessalonians 2:9) "...for we walk by faith, not by sight." (2Corinthians 5:7)* *(Jeremiah 17:14, John 8:36)*

# YOU CAN'T RUN FROM GOD!

**PRINCIPLE:** OUR PRAYERS PURSUE THE ONES WE LOVE, EVEN WHEN WE CANNOT.

After receiving Jesus, my heart ached for my family to know Him. My twin brother, Joseph, came to our Christian community and was baptized but considered it merely a part of his spiritual journey. He left shortly afterward, continuing his quest in Eastern religions.

A few months passed.

One day, Joseph was travelling on a hippie bus through our town. The bus had made a wrong turn and went down a dead end street, right past the home of my pastor, Jerry Russell. When Jerry saw the bus, he thought it might be connected with a Christian community he knew, so he jumped in his car, and on a busy highway, pulled it over. Joseph recognized Jerry, but didn't want to see him, and so hid in the back of the bus while others got out.

Months later, Joseph was back in New York and about to leave for the Far East. He told me the amazing story about Jerry stopping his bus, and so I challenged him that God orchestrated the event. He hung up in anger and went to India and Nepal for a year and half. During that season, for one six-month period, no one in our family had heard from Joseph and we were all quite concerned. So, my sister Maria's husband George, who had also accepted Christ, went on a seven-day fast to pray for Joseph. **At the end of that time of prayer and fasting, while Joseph was meditating on his bed in Delhi, India, a cross illuminated on a wall in his room and Jesus spoke to his heart, "I am the way!"**[6]

A short time later, Joseph returned to the States and was saved.

**God answers prayer!**

---

**SCRIPTURE** *"If I ascend into heaven, You are there; if I make my bed in hell, behold, You are there." (Psalm 139:8, NKJV)*

6. JOHN 14:6

# THE SUPERNATURAL MARKED MY LIFE!

**PRINCIPLE:** WE ARE ETERNAL, SPIRIT BEINGS HAVING A TEMPORARY, NATURAL EXPERIENCE.

We are each made up of a spirit, soul and body. Our spirit is our God-consciousness: where Jesus desires to live. Our soul is our self-consciousness, our mind, will, and emotions: the primary battleground for our inner transformation. Our spirit and soul will live forever, while our body is the temporary shell we inhabit while on Earth.

You and I have never seen anything eternal with our natural eyes. This world is the matrix. The real world is invisible and can only be seen with eyes of faith. So, in order to change the visible realm, we must learn to see into the invisible and the supernatural.

**Since this world is not our final destiny, our goal in life is to discover Heaven's eternal blessings and not be seduced by Earth's temporary distractions.** Frankly, our time here is a dress rehearsal for eternity. Every aspect of life on Earth is a test.[7]

As Jesus prayed to His Father, "Your Kingdom come. Your will be done on earth as it is in heaven."[8] His prayer was heard, and it will be answered. Only Heaven can reveal the best in us. Allow God's supernatural Heaven to come to your natural Earth.

Sadly, many Christians are practical atheists. They believe in God, but for all practical purposes, don't really believe He will do anything supernatural. Even still, God's Word and promises are true! It is impossible for Him to lie[9]. Jesus said, "The Spirit of the Lord is on me, because he has…sent me to proclaim freedom for the prisoners and recovery of sight for the blind, to set the oppressed free…"[10]

**Live the supernatural life, and you will see God do miracles!**

---

**SCRIPTURE** *"If I ascend into heaven, You are there; if I make my bed in hell, behold, You are there." And these signs will accompany those who believe: in my name they will cast out demons; they will speak in new tongues; they will pick up serpents with their hands; and if they drink any deadly poison, it will not hurt them; they will lay their hands on the sick, and they will recover." (Mark 16:17–18)*

7. GOD TESTED THE PATRIARCH JOSEPH: PSALM 105:17–19,
AND KING HEZEKIAH: 2CHRONICLES 32:31
8. LUKE 11:2, NKJV
9. HEBREWS 6:18
10. LUKE 4:18, NIV

# NOTHING'S MORE SUPER-NATURAL THAN WORSHIP

**PRINCIPLE:** PERSONAL AND CORPORATE REVIVALS ARE BIRTHED IN WORSHIP.

---

**We are made to worship! Everyone is worshipping someone or something.**

Be careful what and who you worship. Jesus said, you must, "...love the LORD your God with all your heart, all your soul, and all your mind."[11] But what does that look like? I believe one of the amazing experiences Jesus had perfectly describes true worship. The Bible tells the story in Luke 7. "When a certain immoral woman from that city heard he was eating there, she brought a beautiful alabaster jar filled with expensive perfume. Then she knelt behind him at his feet, weeping. Her tears fell on his feet, and she wiped them off with her hair. Then she kept kissing his feet and putting perfume on them."[12]

Her actions sublimely demonstrated what total, complete, abandoned worship looks like!

**The measure of my gratefulness for what Jesus has done for me is best seen in how I worship Him.**

If you have been born again, then you have experienced the presence of God—and like me, you know God's presence has been the difference between life and death. That's why, when God told Moses in the wilderness, "My presence will go with you..." Moses responded, "If Your Presence does not go with us, do not bring us up from here."[13] Moses was saying 'God, if you're not going with me, then I don't want to go. I already saw that movie, and it didn't end well.'

**Either we let Jesus lead us by His Spirit, or we return to following someone who doesn't know where they're going. Only God knows what is best for me.** I never have, and following Him has been the greatest joy in my life.

---

**SCRIPTURE** *"As soon as Solomon finished his prayer, fire came down from heaven and consumed the burnt offering and the sacrifices, and the glory of the Lord filled the temple. And the priests could not enter the house of the Lord, because the glory of the Lord filled the Lord's house. When all the people of Israel saw the fire come down and the glory of the Lord on the temple, they bowed down with their faces to the ground on the pavement and worshiped and gave thanks to the Lord, saying, "For he is good, for his steadfast love endures forever." (2Chronicles 7:1-3)*

11. LUKE 10:27
12. LUKE 7:37-38
13. EXODUS 33:14-15

# DAY **18**   GIVING AWAY ALL I HAD    1972

**PRINCIPLE:**   THE SOONER WE REALIZE GOD OWNS
EVERYTHING, THE FREER WE'LL BE.

The night before I received Jesus I slept on a river. My only possessions were a backpack and sleeping bag. In the "Jesus Freak" community I lived in at the time, someone needed to borrow a backpack and sleeping bag to visit his family, so I said sure. It's only been 44 years; I'm sure he is still trying to make it back to return my belongings. But freely I had received, and so freely I gave.

Living communally, we only made $2 each week; all of the additional money we earned was pooled to support the community. It became even more challenging when God asked me to give away my first brand new, quality Bible; for which I had saved up, over many months. Ouch!

Then, when believers from Alaska told us how our brothers and sisters were freezing and could really use warm work boots... Hmm? I just happened to have a brand new pair saved up under my bed. There seemed to be pattern; God wanted me to be attached to Him and not my stuff. What I thought was a coincidental sequence at the time has become a lifestyle.

There's a syndrome that some two year olds experience. It's called, "You exist to bless me." Perhaps that's why it's called the "terrible two's." As parents, we know that part of the process of successfully raising children is to transition them from being "natural-born takers" into being "supernatural givers." There's no learning process in "taking." We're all born "master-takers."

**Yet, the only way we can fully experience the greatest fulfillment in life is learning how to give. Though God is a blessing to me, He doesn't exist to bless me. Teaching us to give is not God's way of raising money; it's God's way of raising His children.**

**SCRIPTURE** *"...do good, and lend, hoping for nothing in return..." (Luke 6:35)*

# DAY 19 TREACHEROUS BOAT RIDE ACROSS SAN FRANCISCO BAY

1972

**PRINCIPLE:** IF WE CAN'T TRUST GOD TO PROTECT US, WE CAN'T BE PROTECTED.

Two weeks after giving my life to Jesus, I found myself in a life and death situation. On a cold spring day, I was paddling out to a houseboat in Sausalito, California, in a six-foot long dinghy, when I lost one of my oars. Unable to stop or control the tiny boat due to a strong wind, I drifted ten miles, for well over an hour, all the way across San Francisco Bay to Berkeley.

No other boat was even in sight, and so, if I had capsized, I would have certainly drowned. Having just read in the Gospels about Peter doubting Jesus and sinking in the water,[14] I resolved to trust God to keep me safe while kneeling in prayer.

God did!

Now 44 years later, I have seen His miraculous, protective hand hundreds of times in my life and in the lives of those I love.

**The only life that is truly blessed is the trusting life! Trusting God even when He's not given you everything you had hoped for.**

Trusting God when you can't believe He would allow something tragic to happen to you.

Being fully persuaded, in the midst of terrible disappointment, that in the end you will receive everything He has ever hoped for you, which is infinitely better. On the other side of your trust is a fully trustworthy God.

**Have you trusted Jesus with your life? You'll find, as I did, He will never fail you.**

---

**SCRIPTURE** *"When Jesus woke up, he rebuked the wind and said to the waves, 'Silence! Be still!' Suddenly the wind stopped, and there was a great calm. Then he asked them, 'Why are you afraid? Do you still have no faith?'" (Mark 4:39–40)*

14. MATTHEW 14:29-30

# 1ST MEAL HOME...WHOLE FAMILY PRAYS TO JESUS

**PRINCIPLE:** AT TIMES, AN INVITATION IS ALL THAT'S NEEDED TO LEAD PEOPLE TO JESUS.

When I received Jesus, I knew it was because of my mother's prayers. She was a praying Catholic who, like Cornelius in Acts 10, had prayers that reached God. I was in California at the time, and my family was in New York, so it took a few months before I could get back to visit them.

When I did, it was seismic!

I had left a year earlier, a longhaired walking germ. Now I returned with short hair, no beard, clean clothes, and a pocket Bible. After praying a lengthy prayer over the meal, I concluded by inviting everyone at the table to say the name "Jesus," reverently. One by one each did: mother, sister, brother-in-law, brother, and sister-in-law. They all said His name. Later, each shared how hard it was just to say the name Jesus reverently. It would be a year before they were all soundly converted, but they have followed Jesus ever since.

Do you feel like your prayers for loved ones aren't being answered? Guess what percentage of prayers initiated by God are answered? 100%! What percentage of prayers initiated by us are answered? 0%! Hmm? Sounds like there's a pattern here. The Bible promises, "This is the confidence we have in approaching God: that if we ask anything according to His will, He hears us. And if we know that He hears us—whatever we ask—we know that we have what we asked of Him."

**God has already figured out what's best for every part of your life. Trust Him!**

**Stop asking God to do things that are in your heart, and start asking Him to do what's on His heart. It's the only guaranteed way to get all of your prayers answered.**

**SCRIPTURE** *"Believe in the Lord Jesus, and you will be saved, you and your household." (Acts 16:31)*

15. ACTS 10:4
16. 1JOHN 5:14-15, NIV

# RUNNING TO... AND NOT FROM

**PRINCIPLE:** GOD SEES SUCCESS AND FAILURE DIFFERENTLY THAN WE DO.

One night, when I was a baby Christian, a home nearby caught fire. Our town of 200 only had a volunteer fire department, so I knew it would take a while for a truck and help to arrive. By the time word spread, the house was completely engulfed in flames. Being young and eager to help, I ran to the scene as fast as I could.

When I arrived, I saw that the house on fire belonged to a 90-year-old woman I knew, Mrs. Carney. She was a key figure in praying for the powerful revival that had come to our little country church months before. This only added to my sense of urgency! I imagined this dear lady lying helplessly inside, and so with all of my strength, I lunged aggressively at the front door to kick it open.

In movies, the hero kicks a door open, runs into the burning building and rescues the family in distress. In my case, the door was slightly ajar already so that when I kicked it I was thrown completely off balance. Falling on my side, I hurt my leg. Now, unable to walk, with flames nearby and smoke billowing from the doorway, my only option was to crawl away. I wasn't successful at this either. After a few agonizingly helpless seconds, others finally arrived and pulled me to safety before a wall of the building collapsed.

I was grateful, but thoroughly embarrassed. Instead of being the rescuer, I became the rescued. My humiliation increased when I discovered I had been mistaken; the house on fire was abandoned. The sweet, elderly saint lived next door. **Our greatest failure is in not trying!**

**Are you running to something, or from something? Simply fleeing from darkness won't transform us. We must run toward the light of God if we are to be truly changed. C.S. Lewis wrote, "Sunlight is the great disinfectant."**

**The Bible says, "...if we walk in the light, as He is in the light, we have fellowship with one another, and the blood of Jesus his Son cleanses us from all sin."[17] And, "Do not be overcome by evil, but overcome evil with good."[18] I want to look back on my life and see that I ran toward the call of God, not away from it.**

**SCRIPTURE** *"When Jesus woke up, he rebuked the wind and said to the waves, 'Silence! Be still!' Suddenly the wind stopped, and there was a great calm. Then he asked them, 'Why are you afraid? Do you still have no faith?'" (Mark 4:39–40)*

**PRINCIPLE:** THE SOONER WE STOP THINKING WE KNOW WHAT'S BEST...THE BETTER.

Everyone learns the hard way; some learn the really hard way, and others never learn.

I realized early on that I did not have the gift of wisdom, but I had the gift of interrogation, so I would pepper the wisest people I knew with questions.

In the early days of being a Christ-follower, I was witnessing to man who was pretty drunk outside of a local bar. He was surprisingly compliant and even knelt down on the sidewalk to receive Jesus. I was elated! Immediately, after standing up, he said, "But I'm sorry I have to do this!" He then swirled around and cold cocked a man behind him. This was followed by complete chaos; culminating with a massive bouncer sitting on my new convert's chest and pounding his head repeatedly into the ground. I gradually faded into the woodwork, with much to ponder. It doesn't take much discernment to acknowledge his prayer wasn't completely sincere.

**Every challenge and every opportunity is known by God and used for our ultimate good!** From setbacks to successes, the moment we stop depending on Jesus we become susceptible to deception. Accept nothing at face value. "...for we walk by faith, not by sight."[19] I'm not moved by what I see. I want to allow the inner witness of God's Spirit to guide me. **Every decision we make tests our motives, and in the end we will be judged by the thoughts and intents of our heart.** The Bible says, "But I, the LORD, search all hearts and examine secret motives. I give all people their due rewards, according to what their actions deserve." [20]

"Jesus, guide me through the treacherous waters of testing. You are able to protect me from great errors in judgment!"

**SCRIPTURE** *"Every way of a man is right in his own eyes, but the LORD weighs the heart." (Proverbs 21:2)*

19. 2CORINTHIANS 5:7
20. JEREMIAH 17:10, NLT

# THE BLESSING OF FINANCIAL OBEDIENCE

---

**PRINCIPLE:** GOD DESIGNED GIVING TO BE THE GREATEST ADVENTURE IN LIFE...FAR GREATER THAN RECEIVING.

---

One of the best commitments my wife, Suzie, and I ever made was our foundational conviction to be obedient to God in our finances. We brought this commitment into our marriage in 1975 and have been faithful to God's financial principles throughout our marriage. It has made all of the difference. We believe everything we have belongs to God.

We've held a deep conviction to have so much "obedient seed" in the ground that our harvest would be inevitable. We have always tithed the first 10% of our income to the Lord through our local church. It has never been a point of discussion, just an unwavering conviction. Beyond tithes, we prayerfully give offerings as God directs us, and that requires mutual agreement and great faith. The fruit of this obedience has impacted every part of our lives. Jesus said, "Give, and you will receive. Your gift will return to you in full—pressed down, shaken together to make room for more, running over, and poured into your lap. The amount you give will determine the amount you get back."

**Every person who's a giver is glad when other people are giving.** Every person who, at this point, is a "taker" is evaluating, "Will becoming a giver actually change my life for the better?" "Are the promises of God really true?" "Will He really open the windows of Heaven for me?" "Have the righteous never ever been forsaken?" All these questions can be answered with one scripture. "For God so loved the world that He gave His only begotten Son, that whoever believes in Him should not perish but have everlasting life."

**Because God so loved...He gave. Not just anything, but His Only Son. God's a giver! That's why He gives His best, and that's why those who know Him do the same.**

---

**SCRIPTURE** *"...my God will meet all your needs according to His glorious riches in Christ Jesus." (Philippians 4:19, NIV)*

21. LUKE 6:38, NLT
22. JOHN 3:16, NKJV

**PRINCIPLE:** THE ONLY WAY TO GET GOD'S BEST IS TO GIVE HIM OURS. WE WILL ALWAYS REAP WHAT WE SOW.

**Here's a great goal in life: get as much good seed into the ground as possible!**

Your seed will always determine your harvest, whether good or bad, and we all should expect a harvest. Would you consider a farmer presumptuous for expecting the land he's sowed seed into to bear fruit? Similarly, wouldn't it be absurd to expect a harvest from a piece of land you've sowed nothing into?

All of us are sowing something and we are reaping something as well. I believe it's fair to say, you and I will reap exactly what we have sown. **Embrace the challenges that come your way, and consider your response to them as a seed. Seeing them as appointments or disappointments is always our choice.** Take some time to reflect each day on the seeds you're sowing.

Perhaps you'd like to be rich! It's a great idea...as long as your riches last forever! **Though you can't take riches with you, you can send them on ahead.** John Wesley said, "We should only value things by the price they shall gain in eternity."

The Bible says, "Think about the things of heaven, not the things of earth. For you died to this life, and your real life is hidden with Christ in God."[23] Jesus reminded us of this when He said, "The Kingdom of Heaven is like a treasure that a man discovered hidden in a field. In his excitement, he hid it again and sold everything he owned to get enough money to buy the field."[24]

**The greatest joys in life are eternal.**

---

**SCRIPTURE** *Abraham was willing to give God his first and best: "And Abraham lifted up his eyes and looked, and behold, behind him was a ram, caught in a thicket by his horns. And Abraham went and took the ram and offered it up as a burnt offering instead of his son." (Genesis 22:13)*

23. COLOSSIANS 3:2-3, NLT
24. MATTHEW 13:44, NLT

**PRINCIPLE:** WHATEVER STRATA OF LIFE YOU ARE IN, GOD CAN REACH YOU, IF YOU ARE SINCERELY OPEN.

A few months after I received Jesus, I was playing golf with my older brother Victor on a Beverly Hills golf course. He was boasting about having just been picked up in a silver Rolls Royce that morning for breakfast at Jack Kent Cooke's home.[25] After listening to him for a few holes, I'd had enough! I shot back, "Vic, Jack Kent Cooke's home will be a pup-tent compared to my home in Heaven!" Perhaps my response wasn't biblically accurate, but it brought some eternal reality into our conversation.

Later that summer, Vic and his wife Kathy attended a Full Gospel Businessmen's meeting in New York City. During lunch, a businessman spent two hours telling them about Jesus, without ever touching his food. That day, Vic and Kathy were born again!

Within a few years, they left New York City, worked on building a church in Portland, Oregon, making less than 10% of Vic's previous annual salary. He also spent 23 years as Chairman of the Board of CCLI[26] until his retirement at 80.

**Now, in his mid-80's, like our intercessory mother, Vic spends hours each day in God's presence praying for others.**

---

**SCRIPTURE** *"For consider your calling, brothers: not many of you were wise according to worldly standards, not many were powerful, not many were of noble birth. But God chose what is foolish in the world to shame the wise; God chose what is weak in the world to shame the strong." (1Corinthians 1:26–27)*

25. JACK KENT COOKE (OCTOBER 25, 1912 – APRIL 6, 1997) WAS A CANADIAN ENTREPRENEUR AND FORMER OWNER OF THE WASHINGTON REDSKINS (NFL) AND THE LOS ANGELES LAKERS (NBA). HE WAS WIDELY CONSIDERED TO BE THE GREATEST OWNER IN THE HISTORY OF PROFESSIONAL SPORTS.

26. CHRISTIAN COPYRIGHT LICENSING INTERNATIONAL IS A PRIVATELY OWNED COMPANY THAT WAS CO-FOUNDED IN THE US IN 1988 BY HOWARD RACHINSKI, WHO IS THE PRESIDENT/CEO, AND VICTOR ANFUSO, CHAIRMAN OF THE BOARD. CCLI OFFERS COPYRIGHT LICENSING OF SONGS AND OTHER RESOURCE MATERIALS FOR USE IN CHRISTIAN WORSHIP.

# ARRESTED AND FIRED FOR PREACHING THE GOSPEL

**PRINCIPLE:** THOUGH THE DECISIONS OF OTHERS MAY AFFECT US, HOW WE RESPOND TO THEM WILL DETERMINE IF THEY BENEFIT US OR NOT.

When I had only been a Christ-follower for a little over a year, I was substitute teaching in a high school. During lunch hour, my best friend Bruce and I, also a teacher, would preach the gospel in a park across the street from the school. Things were going well, and as many as 200 students were coming out to hear us. Though the crowd was generally pretty aggressive, one day things really got out of control.

One of the men who came with us, who never preached, was having a conversation with a student. Foolishly he told her that because of all the makeup she wore, she looked like the harlot Jezebel. What!! When her boyfriend heard this man say this to her, he flipped out. A riot ensued. The police were called and all three of us were hauled away, making the front page of the local newspaper. Ouch!! We were then fired from our teaching jobs and given six months' probation.

A great opportunity was lost because of someone's poor judgment. Never in my wildest imaginations would I have thought a fellow believer would say something like that. But once the words were spoken, none of our apologies could get the genie back in the bottle. Now, over 40 years later, it is still sad and embarrassing to think about.

But, we all learned a hard lesson. **Words have consequences. Don't go into battle with someone who is unproven. And, lastly, even though it was a tough pill to swallow, it etched into my soul and spirit how desperately we need God to help us.**

As the Psalmist wrote, "Keep back your servant also from presumptuous sins; let them not have dominion over me! Then I shall be blameless, and innocent of great transgression."[27]

**SCRIPTURE** *"Above all, keep loving one another earnestly, since love covers a multitude of sins." (1Peter 4:8) "Most of all, love each other as if your life depended on it. Love makes up for practically anything." (1Peter 4:8, The Message)*

27. PSALM 19:13

# MY TENDER HEARTED TWIN

**PRINCIPLE:** THE MOST INSPIRING THING YOU AND I CAN BE IS "ALL IN!"

Is there anything more impacting than a changed life? It's actually irrefutable!

There is not a person I'm more proud of than my twin brother, Joseph. He's a transformed man! Always an adventurer, and more aggressive than me, I grew up saying, "Joseph don't!" He was willing to do the unthinkable...often dangerous, always outside the box! Most people wouldn't consider me conservative, but compared to Joseph I was a monk.

His exploits are renowned. Arrested at 16 for sneaking out late one night and driving a sports car 120 miles an hour in just his underwear. Running to swing from a vine over a jungle ravine in Hawaii, realizing all too late it was attached to nothing. Climbing to the base camp of Mount Everest, 18,192 feet, without a sleeping bag or tent. Arriving at sunset on the frozen glacier, and walking back to his campsite under a full moon, arriving at 3 A.M. Elsewhere in the Himalayas, Joseph was chased and captured by Nepalese soldiers as he tried to sneak past their sentry post. He then brazenly exited the cell they'd thrown him in, and walked away, while guards continued to yell and threaten him.

But once Joseph surrendered his heart to Jesus, the real legacy of his life began. He founded a Christian Relief and Missions Organization called Forward Edge in 1983. Since then, Joseph has worked with others to rescue dozens of young girls from forced prostitution in a garbage dump in Nicaragua. He's sent thousands of volunteers around the world to help victims of earthquakes, hurricanes, typhoons, and tsunamis, all in the name of Jesus Christ.

**If there's a catastrophe where the love of God is needed, Joseph's all in.** Every time I talk to him about his Christ-centered adventures we cry together.

His tender heart inspires me! **God likewise created you to be an adventurer for Him. Perhaps not as "out there" as Joseph, but inspired by your Creator just the same.**

---

**SCRIPTURE** "...my God will meet all your needs according to His glorious riches in Christ Jesus." (Philippians 4:19, NIV)

# MIRACLE IN A WYOMING BLIZZARD

**PRINCIPLE:** THERE IS NO ONE WHO WANTS TO PROTECT YOU MORE THAN GOD.

One of the greatest miracles I ever experienced took place as a young Christian. I was driving across the northern U.S. in the middle of December with a young couple, in a tiny, compact car. The wife was eight months pregnant. One night, we found ourselves in a blinding blizzard in a remote part of Wyoming. The cold and wind was so severe it stalled our car. Thinking we'd pulled off the highway sufficiently, the husband and I got out, leaving the expectant mom in the back seat.

All of a sudden, with no driver, the car rolled forward, further off the road, about ten feet. Immediately, an 18-wheeler came barreling past us, missing the car by inches. We all knew God had saved our lives.

Are you sure of God's heart for you? Are you fully persuaded there's nothing He wouldn't do to come to your rescue? The Bible calls this kind of confidence in God "faith." It pleases God because when we are confident in Him, it shows we truly understand His heart. The Bible says, "Faith is the confidence that what we hope for will actually happen."[28]

**It's been said that you pan for gold when you're not sure how much is there, but you mine for gold when you hit a vein. Don't spend your life panning for what you are not sure even exists. Reach out to your Creator and receive His love.** Ask Jesus to come into your heart and fill your life with the eternal treasures He's prepared because He loves you so very much.

**Can you remember a time when God rescued you?**

**SCRIPTURE** *"My God, my rock, in whom I take refuge, my shield, and the horn of my salvation, my stronghold and my refuge, my savior; you save me from violence. I call upon the Lord, who is worthy to be praised, and I am saved from my enemies."* *(2Samuel 22:3-4)*

28. HEBREWS 11:1, NLT

# SUZIE SURRENDERS AND BECOMES A DISCIPLE

**PRINCIPLE:** VIEWING THE BACK OF OUR LIFE QUILT REVEALS THE BRILLIANCE OF GOD'S WILL.

God orders each of our lives in such supernatural ways. Only in retrospect can we see His divine guidance. Some of this eternal sequencing will be revealed in eternity. Others will stand out as milestones of God's sacred symmetry.

In 1974, I produced a multi-media presentation of music and preaching, called "The Purpose and Vision of God." Suzie attended it and was so impacted that she drove home in her sports car crying. Stirred and challenged to her core the next day she called one of her spiritual leaders and said she had made a deeper commitment to follow Jesus. Suzie wanted to be a whole-hearted follower of Jesus. It was a turning point in her life! How providential that my wife-to-be would be impacted by something I created. Within 18 months we would fall in love and get married. **Looking back, my heavenly Father not only ordered my steps, but also Suzie's. It was another miraculous milestone that would mark both of our lives.**

All of us need a life and death operation, an open-heart surgery... giving entrance to our heart and spirit, to God Himself. "Then he (Jesus) said to them all: 'Whoever wants to be my disciple must deny themselves and take up their cross daily and follow me.'"[29] Unless we are willing, God will never force us to love or follow Him. But if we are open and surrender our heart to Him, we can have an eternal love relationship with the God of the Universe.

So, what will you decide? Will you let Jesus have your heart? Will you become His disciple? Will you receive His promise? "I will give you a new heart, and a new spirit I will put within you. And I will remove the heart of stone from your flesh and give you a heart of flesh."[30]

---

**SCRIPTURE** *"As Jesus passed on from there, he saw a man called Matthew sitting at the tax booth, and he said to him, 'Follow me.' And he rose and followed him."* *(Matthew 9:9)*

29. LUKE 9:23, NIV
30. EZEKIEL 36:26

## SUZIE'S HUSBAND DIES IN A PLANE CRASH

**PRINCIPLE:** GOD ALWAYS HAS A WONDERFUL "NEXT" FOR US, IF WE'RE WILLING TO TRUST HIM.

In the spring of 1974, two years after my conversion, I volunteered to help plant a church in South Lake Tahoe, California. It was there I fell head-over-heels in love with my beautiful wife, Suzie. Her first marriage had been to her high school sweetheart. After Suzie became a Christian, she prayed for him to receive Jesus, but to no avail. Tragically, on the day he was going to file for divorce, he was killed flying a single engine plane.

At that time, Suzie was living in the sisters' dorm in our Christian community. Around midnight on the day of his fatal accident, her dad and mom came to break the news to her. Sobbing quietly, she went into her dorm room to pack some clothes. A scripture on the wall above the bed caught her eye. It was a New Testament verse that would become pivotal, not just for Suzie's life, but for mine as well. Romans 8:28 says, "And we know that for those who love God all things work together for good, for those who are called according to his purpose."

As the truth of this hope-filled scripture entered her heart, a calming peace gave her inner confidence God had everything under control. Within six months, she had joined our church planting team in Lake Tahoe, and a short while later we fell in love. **God had brought both of our dysfunctional lives full circle.**

Suzie and I were married on November 1, 1975, and have spent our lives giving hope to the hopeless, loving the seemingly unlovable, and watching God restore thousands of broken lives.

**Only by allowing God to heal us, can we realize our true destiny: helping others get healed in the same way God healed us.**

**SCRIPTURE** *"For everything there is a season, and a time for every matter under heaven. A time to be born, and a time to die..." (Ecclesiastes 3:1-2a)*

# INSULTING A NEW YORK CITY ICON

**PRINCIPLE:** EVEN WHEN WE MESS UP, GOD CAN USE UNLIKELY VESSELS TO ACCOMPLISH HIS WILL.

My older brother Victor's wife, Kathy, was the daughter of William Shea, of Shea Stadium fame. He built one of New York's largest and most influential law firms, and was instrumental in bringing the New York Mets and National League Baseball back to the city.

In 1973, while visiting my family in New York, I found myself alone with Bill Shea. As a fledgling Christ-follower, I thought I'd tackle the #1 issue in his life, and said, "It is easier for a camel to go through the eye of a needle than for a rich person to enter the kingdom of God."[31] A gracious man, he tried to share some of the many charities he supported, but I continued to aggressively drive my point home.

**Soon after, I realized my approach was completely inappropriate, and was not surprised he made sure he was never alone with me again.**

Years later, one of Victor and Kathy's children, Victor Thomas, would pray and cry every night, "My grandma and grandpa have to be in Heaven with me!" He did this for months. In 1984, his grandparents came to visit Victor and Kathy and their children. Victor Thomas (VT) was 11 years old. I had written a booklet entitled, Are You Going To Heaven? It presented a simple gospel message. VT got a hold of it and spent weeks, painstakingly memorizing every word in order to share it with his grandparents. He did this, even though he had significant neurological disabilities.

As soon as they arrived, even before they brought in their luggage, VT pulled them into the back yard saying, "I need to talk to you!" **He then took them through the booklet and they both prayed to receive Jesus. From that point on they began to read the Bible. An unlikely vessel had been used by God to make an eternal difference.**

**SCRIPTURE** *"...the foolishness of God is wiser than men, and the weakness of God is stronger than men." (1Corinthians 1:25)*

31. MARK 10:25

# WHO WE ARE IN PRIVATE... IS WHO WE ARE

**PRINCIPLE:** IN THE END, THERE'S NO SECRET IN OUR HEART THAT OUR CONDUCT WILL NOT REVEAL.

The saddest experiences I've ever had as a Christian leader are being called into crisis situations after a leader has fallen. There have been more than I care to remember. One tragic scenario was with a pastor who, after a moral failure late in his life, went from caring for thousands of people to caring for thousands of bags of potato chips. It was crushing to see the devastation in his family. To say the least, it put the fear of God in me.

**Are you searching for that which satisfies for a moment, or that which lasts forever?**

Never underestimate deception's ability to embrace a false concept as an absolute truth—to explain away the simplicity of God's reality. I am unable to present my life as more whole than I really am. This would make me no better than the Pharisees of old. My only honest option is to acknowledge the obvious: I am a flawed man desperately in need of a gracious Savior to rescue me and an all wise Lord to rule over my soul and spirit. In order for this to happen **I must turn myself in daily, living a transparent life that embarrasses and costs me the most.** I must do all I can to undo the false premise that as a leader I am inherently less of a sinner and more of a saint than those I serve. The ground is level at the Cross. I must kneel at the feet of Jesus, finding the forgiveness and strength to not live a lie, saying words that cost me nothing. He gave His all, and so must I.

An NFL football player provides each of us an excellent example of the level of integrity followers of Jesus should have, even in private. He said, "When I'm working out alone, I expect every bit as much from myself as I do when coaches or teammates or workout partners are watching. No shortcuts. No cheating. No manipulating. No rationalizing. I know that nobody's watching. I know that no one would ever know... I want to know I have done everything I needed to do to prepare myself... I can allow no shortcuts, not even in private."

**This sounds like a great goal for each of us.
Who I am in private...is who I am!**

**SCRIPTURE** *"Nothing in all creation is hidden from God's sight. Everything is uncovered and laid bare before the eyes of him to whom we must give account."* *(Hebrews 4:13, NIV)*

# PROPOSING TO SUZIE . . . PROMISING FIDELITY

**PRINCIPLE:** GOD IS THE ORIGINAL PROMISE KEEPER, WHO NEVER MAKES A PLEDGE HE DOESN'T KEEP, FROM NOW UNTO ETERNITY.

When I married my wife Suzie in November 1975, I made a commitment to be faithful to her. I even wrote and sang a song on our wedding day with the chorus, "Suzie, I won't fail you! Come draw near!" Why did I write this? Because I had not been a faithful man before committing my life to Jesus in 1972. I was reassuring myself, and Suzie, that I intended to be true to her all the days of her life. Though I had little confidence in myself, I believed God would give me the strength I needed. Now, over 40 years later, I've found my failures don't define me. Instead, by receiving God's forgiving grace, "I know the one in whom I trust, and I am sure that he is able to guard what I have entrusted to him until the day of his return."[32]

**But, how can any of us hope to be faithful? What is it going to take to make us the people of integrity we know we should be?**

There was a famous line at the end of a movie where a man finally admits he loves a woman and says, "You complete me!" Wow! That's romantic! Sensational! It'll make you cry! But it's just not true! I love my wife dearly, and she loves me. But I don't complete her, and she doesn't complete me. **Unless you and I find our completeness in the God who created us, we'll never be complete.** In the Book of Colossians, the Bible is crystal clear, "We are complete in Him (in Jesus)."[33]

**I've seen people try to find the integrity they long for in everything imaginable, but there's only one thing that works: a daily relationship with Jesus Christ.**

**SCRIPTURE** *"He is the faithful God who keeps His covenant for a thousand generations and lavishes His unfailing love on those who love Him and obey His commands." (Deuteronomy 7:9, NLT)*

32. 2TIMOTHY 1:12, NLT
33. COLOSSIANS 2:10

## HEARST CASTLE COWARDICE

**PRINCIPLE:** LEARNING TO HATE COWARDICE WILL BE A TURNING POINT IN OUR LIVES.

On our honeymoon, in November of 1975, my wife, Suzie and I toured the estate of newspaper magnate William Randolph Hearst in San Simeon, California. During his lifetime, celebrities and politicians frequented the opulent mansion with its swimming pools, great halls, extravagant architecture, paintings and lavish antiques. Having been raised in a family that pursued materialism, I had rejected accumulating "stuff" as a worthy pursuit, even before I received Jesus.

So, after a couple of hours, as I was drowning in the "OOHH'S & AAHH'S" of those touring, our bus headed out of the grounds past the private zoo. I was done!

The closing sentence by our bus driver over the P.A. got my complete attention. "Does anyone have a question?" Immediately, the Holy Spirit reminded me of this scripture. "What does it profit if a man gains the whole world and loses his soul?"[34]

It was a lightning bolt of reality, piercing the shallowness of the past two hours. No one had any questions.

The bus wound its way down. Minutes passed. The words were in my mouth, but never came out. I staggered off the bus, knowing I had missed a golden opportunity.

It's still a haunting memory.

**But, it did become the fuel for hundreds of other divinely crafted sentences and opportunities to follow. I had struck out, but singles, doubles, triples and even home runs were ahead.**

**I hate cowardice in me! I refuse to bow and be intimidated! "Jesus, help me to represent you well every moment of my life."**

---

**SCRIPTURE** *"For what will it profit a man if he gains the whole world and forfeits his soul? Or what shall a man give in return for his soul?" (Matthew 16:26)*

34. MATTHEW 16:26

# THE EVANGELISTIC YEARS

*1976–1984*

# THE EVANGELISTIC YEARS

*1972–1975*

OUR TWIN DAUGHTERS: HAVILAH, DEBORAH, AND MY BEAUTIFUL WIFE, SUZIE

MY MOTHER'S PRAYER LEGACY

MY MOTHER, THE INTERCESSOR

MOM'S 75TH BIRTHDAY WITH FIVE CHILDREN: FRANCIS, DIANA, MARIA, JOSEPH AND VICTOR

JOSEPH LIVING ON THE EDGE, RESCUING CHILDREN

## ASKING GIRLFRIEND'S FATHER FOR FORGIVENESS

**PRINCIPLE:** ONE OF THE MOST COURAGEOUS THINGS WE CAN EVER DO IS ASK FORGIVENESS.

When I was newly married, my wife and I went to a seminar that encouraged us to make things right with people in our past. I was convicted about one person in particular: my ex-girlfriend's father. He was a straight-laced New York City firefighter. I was a fledgling hippie. He wouldn't even let me enter his home until I cut my hair. So, after much struggle, I cut most of my hair off, put it in a paper bag, and unannounced, walked into his house during breakfast and arrogantly dropped the bag on his kitchen table. I was a real jerk.

Some five years later, I was now a Christ-follower and challenged by the Holy Spirit to call and ask forgiveness. When he answered the phone, I told him I had become a Christian, and that God had challenged me to ask his forgiveness. After what seemed a long pause, he forgave me saying, "We all make mistakes... etc." He ended by sincerely thanking me for the call. It was an embarrassing and extremely difficult call, but one I'm so glad I made.

It reminds me much of walking. **Walking is actually learning to correct a continuous state of imbalance. Walking, like life, is a constant mid-course correction. Our continuous adjustment is saying, "I was heading in the wrong direction, but now I'm getting back on track." "I was wrong, but I want to make it right."**

Isn't it funny, that after all of the times we've blown it in our lives, we still have trouble admitting when we're wrong? Admitting we're wrong is actually very healing. It's truly one of the most positive things we can do.

No one begins by mastering the "art of walking." **Our first steps in life are always wobbly and unstable. But, as time goes by, our walk becomes steady. Eventually... we can even carry others.**

**SCRIPTURE** *"So if you are offering your gift at the altar and there remember that your brother has something against you, leave your gift there before the altar and go. First be reconciled to your brother, and then come and offer your gift." (Matthew 5:23-24)*

# WHEREVER I AM IN THE WORLD, I'LL COME TO YOU

**PRINCIPLE:** IF WE WILL TRUST HIM, GOD TRULY IS THE GOD OF HAPPY ENDINGS.

When my wife, Suzie, and I had been married for just nine months, I went to Montreal, Quebec to film Christians publicly sharing their faith outside the 1976 Olympic venues.

The day before the Olympics were to begin, I called home and found out the doctor had just told Suzie, now three months pregnant, that she was probably having a miscarriage. The news was jarring! We prayed and I offered to take the next plane back to California, but she insisted I stay. My courageous wife, knowing how important the filming was to me, was resolute that I did not need to return home and that she would be fine.

But after praying further and getting counsel, on the day the Olympics started and filming began, after months of grueling preparation, I found myself boarding a plane—doing the right thing—but hating every minute of it. I was mad. I loved my wife, and wanted to be there for her, but why did God have to pick one of the most important events in my young Christian life to ask for my obedience? His timing seemed, to say the least, really lousy!

We did suffer the loss of our first precious baby through miscarriage. It was a sad and painful loss, but a gigantic statement had been made. A pillar was put in place that remains steadfast throughout more than 40 years of marriage. **Wherever I am in the world, whatever work I am doing, if Suzie needs me, I will drop everything else and come to her side.**

One year later, God graciously gave us two beautiful, identical twin daughters.

**For God so loved...He gave....**

---

**SCRIPTURE** *God will give us "...beauty for ashes, the oil of joy for mourning, the garment of praise for the spirit of heaviness; that [we]...may be called trees of righteousness, the planting of the Lord, that He may be glorified." (Isaiah 61:3, NKV)*

# LEADING BOXING KNOCKOUT KING TO JESUS

**PRINCIPLE:** GREAT VICTORIES OFTEN FOLLOW GREAT SETBACKS.

As I shared in the previous devotional, my filming at the 1976 Montreal Olympics was cut short by my wife Suzie having symptoms of a miscarriage. But God had an incredible divine appointment prepared for me on my flight home.

Being greatly disappointed to be flying home the day the Olympics were starting, I was trying to jumpstart my heart by reading the Bible. A large, distinguished, middle-aged black man, dressed in an African shirt and hat, interrupted me, and began to ask me questions about the Bible. It led to a two-hour conversation and him receiving Jesus.

His name was Archie Moore. I found out later he had been the former Light Heavyweight Boxing Champion of the world who holds the all-time knockout record. He even fought, and almost defeated, the legendary Rocky Marciano for the Heavyweight title. "Archie Moore was the oldest boxer to win the world's Light Heavyweight crown, and is believed to be the only boxer to have boxed professionally in the eras of Joe Louis, Rocky Marciano and Cassius Clay/Muhammad Ali. He was one of a handful of boxers whose careers spanned four decades, and he had a final record of 186 wins, with 145 official knockout wins."[35]

How ironic! **Having been knocked out of filming at the Olympics, I had the privilege of leading to Christ a future Hall of Fame boxer with the most knockouts in history.**

I left the plane more at peace than I had been in the previous 24 hours; humbled that, even in the middle of my struggle for understanding, God could still use me to impact the life of this man. I was flying high, having obeyed God and seen immediate fruit. **There is life after failure!**

SCRIPTURE *"More than that, we rejoice in our sufferings, knowing that suffering produces endurance, and endurance produces character, and character produces hope, and hope does not put us to shame, because God's love has been poured into our hearts through the Holy Spirit who has been given to us." (Romans 5:3–5)*

35. ACCORDING TO THE INTERNET ENCYCLOPEDIA WIKIPEDIA

# CARING FOR MY DYING PASTOR

**PRINCIPLE:** LIFE'S CLOSEST FRIENDSHIPS CAN BE WITH PEOPLE WE'VE STRUGGLED WITH MOST.

In 1974, I was the worship leader on a team planting a new church in South Lake Tahoe, California. Our pastor, Rick Carlson, was a former Army Ranger in Vietnam who, prior to his conversion, had been the largest drug dealer in Yuba County, California. We were both strong-willed choleric men, who clashed regularly. After about 15 months, Suzie and I felt led to go back to our home church, in preparation for our marriage.

A year later, Rick was battling cancer, and in the final stages he contacted me, of all people, to come and take care of him. I was married by then. So, Suzie and I went to live with Rick, his wife, Angela, and their three children. For the next month, my relationship with him morphed into one of the closest friendships I've ever had. I took care of him, loved him, held his hand, carried him to the bathroom, cleaned up his vomit, and was the last person to pray with him before he died. **Next to my earthly father and mother, there is no one I long to see more in Heaven than my friend, Rick.**

Who in your life is presently far from you that God may send your way in the days ahead? Someone you would least expect; God could use you to touch his or her life. All you need to do at this time is be open. **You might be surprised what dead ends are actually invitations to off-road experiences that will change you forever.**

As the songwriter wrote, "There's a land that is fairer than day, and by faith we can see it afar; for the Father waits over the way to prepare us a dwelling place there. In the sweet by and by, we shall meet on that beautiful shore."

**SCRIPTURE** *"Then they also will answer, saying, 'Lord, when did we see you hungry or thirsty or a stranger or naked or sick or in prison, and did not minister to you?'" (Matthew 25:44)*

36. SANFORD F. BENNETT, 1868

# EVEL KNIEVEL TEACHING KIDS TO ROLLER-SKATE

**PRINCIPLE:** NEVER SAY "NEVER!" TO GOD.
HIS WILL IS OFTEN COUNTER INTUITIVE.

Over time, the Christian community I had been saved in lost its way. Some 75 people were still living at Morning Star, in Smartsville, but the leadership had gotten off into an "extreme grace" doctrine. Some people were involved in immoral acts (sex and drugs), and no correction was being given. Something had to be done, or the community would continue to disintegrate into complete deception.

My father-in-the-Lord, Jerry Russell, asked me to be the pastor of the community for a maximum of six to nine months. I thought the request was absurd. I was an ordained evangelist, not a pastor. I respectfully shared with him these words, "It's like asking Evel Knievel to teach Sunday School kids to roller skate." He was not deterred, and followed with, "The Bible doesn't say, 'The Lord is my Evangelist.' It says, 'The Lord is my Shepherd.' You aren't going to go very far in God without a shepherd's heart."

**WOW! Convicting, God-inspired words! So, off we went.**

By then, the community had so deteriorated that when I read the rules to all present, one man in the back openly shook his fist at me. It would be a very difficult, periodically life-threatening, experience lasting four years and four months...52 months to the day.

**The pressures and struggles I would experience prepared me for the decades to come.** In the Message version of the book of James the brother of Jesus, who was later martyred for his faith, says, "Consider it a sheer gift, friends, when tests and challenges come at you from all sides. You know that under pressure, your faith-life is forced into the open and shows its true colors. So don't try to get out of anything prematurely. Let it do its work so you become mature and well-developed, not deficient in any way."[37]

**SCRIPTURE** *"The steps of a good man are ordered by the Lord.'" (Psalm 37:23, NKJV)*

37. JAMES 1:2-3, THE MESSAGE

**PRINCIPLE:** IF WE'RE READY TO DIE FOR OUR FAITH, WE WON'T BE AFRAID OF ANYONE OR ANYTHING.

My life was threatened on many occasions when I pastored the Morning Star community. For four years and four months, we ministered to dozens of individuals struggling with addictions to drugs and alcohol. Though we were fully committed to helping people, lying and deception was not tolerated. It was often a deal breaker. The first time I asked a man, his wife, and two children to leave the community, it was because he was sneaking and doing drugs. He got so irate, as I walked away with my pastor, he yelled, "I'm going to kill you!" My pastor immediately whispered, "Don't take it personally." Wise advice, though it sounded somewhat ridiculous at the time.

Another incident occurred in my counseling office that directly connected to my house where I lived with my wife and baby twin daughters. I was counseling a man who, while crying hysterically, confessed to killing six people, including blowing his uncle out a window with a 12-gauge shotgun. During our meeting, he got so enraged at me, he put his fist through the sheetrock right next to my head. **On this and many similar occasions I found I had to accept the fact that though my life could be taken at any point, I refused to bow in fear.**

Though we saw many people set free, some could not cut loose their attachment to their drug of choice. In The Great Divorce, C. S. Lewis chronicles the battle many go through with addictions. He describes a busload of people from Hell who tour the outskirts of Heaven. Each person is urged to leave his sin behind. Sadly, they express denial and self-delusion about their addictions. Though miserable, they blame others and pity themselves, refusing to take responsibility for their behavior or see the root of their problems.

The Bible encourages us, "Blessed is the man who remains steadfast under trial, for when he has stood the test he will receive the crown of life..."[38]

**SCRIPTURE** *Jesus said, "And do not fear those who kill the body but cannot kill the soul. Rather fear him who can destroy both soul and body in hell." (Matthew 10:28) and did not minister to you?"' (Matthew 25:44)*

38. JAMES 1:12A

# SUZIE'S FAMILY RECEIVES JESUS

**PRINCIPLE:** HAVING FAITH FOR OUR FAMILY'S SALVATION MAY BE THEIR TURNING POINT.

**There is no shelf life for Spirit anointed prayers.**

As I had a praying mother, Suzie had a praying grandma, her mom's mother. Grandma Clawson had once agreed in prayer with her pastors for Suzie's salvation. Eventually the dominoes fell. Suzie was the first to become a Christian. Next came her brothers, Joe and Rob, and their wives, Becky and Karen. And then Suzie's mother, who had been backslidden for 50 years, gave her heart to Jesus at midnight kneeling in her living room, on her husband's birthday.

Eventually, many children, and children's children would grow up and make decisions to follow Jesus. **A generational blessing in Suzie's family continues to this day, now in the fifth generation.**

Day 35 devotional mentions my filming in Montreal. The day after Suzie's disconcerting doctor's appointment about miscarrying our baby, she had gone to stay with her parents for emotional support. I knew she was not expecting me to return so soon. However, I decided not to call but to surprise her. She was shocked to see me standing there with flowers. Bursting into tears, we hugged and cried. It was a very moving moment. Even her dad, an atheist who rarely showed emotion, choked up when he greeted me, and looking into my eyes he said, "Son, you did the right thing!"

I have no doubt, many years later when Dad finally gave his heart to Jesus, that some of the first seeds of trust were sown on that fateful day. As her father, he didn't care if a video of the Olympics was made or not.

**What he did care about was that his daughter's husband was willing to give up even the most important thing he was doing to come to her aid.**

**People will see far more of God in us by how we respond to failure than to success.**

---

**SCRIPTURE** *And they said, "Believe in the Lord Jesus, and you will be saved, you and your household." (Acts 16:31)*

# DAY 42 SUZIE'S GIFT IN NURTURING CHILDREN

**PRINCIPLE:** WE HAVE NO GREATER TREASURE OR INHERITANCE THAN OUR CHILDREN.

**Suzie and I had only been married for a few years when a Christian leader challenged me for not listening to my wife.** He said to her, prophetically and publicly, "Your husband, because of his strength, doesn't listen to you. But God's going to dig in his ear, because He's given you great wisdom." It was a huge wake-up call! I'd been overpowering my wife with words our entire marriage. I didn't realize that godly wives are given an intuitive sensitivity, and as husbands we need to draw from this reservoir of God-given wisdom. In Proverbs, when God speaks of wisdom, it is in a feminine context. He says, "She / wisdom calls aloud..."[39]

When it came to raising children, Suzie was a savant, which literally means "a knowing person." She just knew how to connect with children. **Both our children and grandchildren have been the beneficiaries of her tireless, loving, patient and intuitive heart.** In the early years of our daughter's lives, she would pull me aside saying, "Honey, I wouldn't say it or do it quite that way."

It was a gentle reproof that I soon followed and came to rely upon.

Why do ostriches bury their heads in the sand? Is it because they are trying to hide and run away from a fight? Hardly! It's actually because they're turning their eggs. They are taking care of their family. They are nurturing the next generation. **In the most distracted age of all time, we should never feel we are wasting our time being present and caring for our children and grandchildren.** The Bible says, God "...gave his instructions to Israel. He commanded our ancestors to teach them to their children, so the next generation might know them—even the children not yet born—and they in turn will teach their own children."[40]

**One of the best ways we can rescue our children from harm is to be present and vigilant in their lives.**

---

**SCRIPTURE** *"For the gifts and the calling of God are irrevocable." (Romans 11:29)*

39. PROVERBS 1:20
40. PSALM 78:5–6, NLT

# MY MOTHER, THE INTERCESSOR

**PRINCIPLE:** WHENEVER SOMEONE RECEIVES JESUS, SOMEONE ELSE WAS PRAYING.

Early church history tells the story of James, the half-brother of Jesus. He was such a man of prayer, his knees had thick calluses, making them look like the knees of a camel. James once wrote, "...pray for one another, that you may be healed. The effective, fervent prayer of a righteous man avails much."[41]

My mother was an intercessor. She stood alone, calling out for the broken lives of her husband, children, and hundreds more. Facing many challenges in her young life, she was driven to the only One who could help. A young wife, with an unfaithful, yet gifted, husband, she shared her dilemma with her father. He quipped, "Does he beat you? Does he give you money?"

She could have fatalistically accepted her abandoned position. Instead, in time, she took her plight to a high power: a perfect Father and Husband, who would become the Love of her life. Day after day, week after week, she prayed. Soon hundreds of names were added to her list. It grew so long, she prayed for the saved one day and the unsaved the next; but for her children, daily. Four hours a day, every day, she'd say in her thick New York accent, "I'm praying my brains out!"

And so she did! I know her prayers had power, because I received Jesus on Mother's Day, 1972.

Mom's prayer book tells the story; the worn pages of a willing life. No one who knew her doubted the power of her appeals. Now, decades later, all of her children still know Jesus, and we call her, "blessed." Each of us is learning to intercede in our own right for those we love. But the question can be rightly asked, "Where are the intercessors? Where are the warrior hearts who wrestle with God for the souls of men?"

Raise them up, oh God, for we so need them now!

---

**SCRIPTURE** *"Then she lived as a widow to the age of eighty-four. She never left the Temple but stayed there day and night, worshiping God with fasting and prayer."* *(Romans 11:29)*

41. JAMES 5:16, NKJV

# LIFE THREATENING PHONE CALL AT 3 A.M.

**PRINCIPLE:** BEING CAUGHT OFF GUARD BY FEAR, IF PROCESSED WITH FAITH, CAN ULTIMATELY MAKE US MORE FEARLESS.

I once led a heroin addict and his wife to the Lord. Within a few months, his body collapsed from years of physical abuse, and he died. I was exhausted from going back and forth to the hospital and ministering to his family, and I went to sleep anticipating his funeral the next day.

At 3 A.M., my phone rang. A man screaming curse words greeted me. He was saying he was going to kill me at the funeral. It was the crazy uncle of the man who had just died. He had recently gotten out of prison, and I knew he was capable of carrying out his threat.

Now, I've had my life threatened many times, but this was different. I'd been awakened out of a dead sleep, completely worn out. With no time to sequence a mental defense to this verbal assault, my knees literally began to knock together. When I went back to bed my wife held me and prayed. I just shook and tried to regroup.

After a long night of prayer, I refused to bow to fear, and so stationed myself at the door of the funeral home. When the uncle came in, I reached out my hand to shake his. He cursed, slapped my hand away, and kept walking. **But I had faced and overcome my fear.**

**Faith and fear have one thing in common; neither one has happened yet. No one can superimpose either filter on how I process my life. I can expect a blessing or curse. I can wrap my arms around the truth or snuggle with lies.**

The Bible says, "In all circumstances take up the shield of faith, with which you can extinguish all the flaming darts of the evil one..."[42]

**No weapon formed against me will prosper...unless I choose to let it. [43] Faith or fear, it's always our choice.**

---

**SCRIPTURE** *"You will not fear the terror of the night, nor the arrow that flies by day..."* (Psalm 91:5)

42. EPHESIANS 6:16
43. ISAIAH 54:17

# MY NEAR NERVOUS BREAKDOWN

**PRINCIPLE:** IT IS NOTHING SHORT OF AMAZING, HOW GOD USES OUR LOWEST MOMENTS TO PROVIDE THE GREATEST INSIGHTS.

In 1981, God was guiding Suzie and me to leave our home church to join an outreach church and fulfill the ministry call on our lives. Desiring to receive the blessing of the Lord, and honor the spiritual authority in our lives, we made a luncheon appointment to share our decision with our pastor. It went well, and he said he would bless us as we went.

Unfortunately, as he was advanced in years, within a short while he either forgot what he had told us, or changed his mind. Initially, he shared in an elder's meeting my intention to leave in a completely derogatory way. I was stunned and deeply hurt. His convictions even spilled over into a public church service, as I sat there with my wife and young children. He said, "Francis is ambitious, and so he is leaving!" WOW! The public humiliation was overwhelming! It sent me in an emotional tailspin that lasted for months. I would drive around our city listening to worship music, crying uncontrollably. At times, fearing for my safety, I would have to pull the car over.

Finally, desperate, I called my father in the Lord, Jerry Russell, at two o'clock in the morning. Upon answering the phone, he said, "I'm so glad you called!" as if he had been awake, waiting for my call. It was beyond reassuring.

We met the next day, and he said something that changed my life. **"Francis, if someone wants the will of God more than anything else, it is impossible for them to miss it." What a word! It set me free!** That's all I wanted, and my heavenly Father would guide me through the process. He did, and the blessing and favor of God went with us.

**SCRIPTURE** *"And after the wind an earthquake, but the Lord was not in the earthquake. And after the earthquake a fire, but the Lord was not in the fire. And after the fire the sound of a low whisper. And when Elijah heard it, he wrapped his face in his cloak and went out and stood at the entrance of the cave.'" (1Kings 19:11b–13a)*

"GOD, WHY IS IT ALWAYS SO HARD?"

**PRINCIPLE:** DON'T BE SURPRISED IF THE POINT IN WHICH YOU'RE CLOSEST TO FULFILLING YOUR DESTINY IS SIMULTANEOUSLY THE LOWEST POINT IN YOUR LIFE.

One night in 1981, at two o'clock in the morning, I was driving home exhausted from trying to launch the evangelistic ministry later known as Christian Equippers International. I was sobbing, overwhelmed by the pressures of life. I cried out to God, "Why does it always have to be so hard?" His response was immediate. Gently, but clearly, He spoke to my heart. "To keep you humble."

All of us would like our lives to be easier. Yet, as I look back over my life, my consistent appeals have not fallen on deaf ears due to indifference; the all-knowing, all-caring God has merely dismissed my fleeting appeals as narrow-minded, showing lack of foresight. **He knows the easy life would destroy my potential; therefore, He makes my life purposefully challenging.**

Only by pressing the olive is the oil poured out; only by crushing the flower is the true fragrance released. Only as Paul and his companions were "pressed out of measure... insomuch that we despaired even of life"[44] did they experience the "sweet-smelling aroma (and become) an acceptable sacrifice, well pleasing to God."[45]

**Have you been saying, "God, why is this happening to me?" A better question would be, "God, what are you trying to show me?"** God is always trying to show us something of eternal value. Paul the Apostle assures us that "...it is God who works in you both to will and to do for His good pleasure." [46]

I once heard some jolting news that could have been received as sad and disappointing. But God in his mercy quickly reminded me of my only responsibility. I am only in charge of the Respond Well Department. He is in charge of everything else.

**SCRIPTURE** *"Humble yourselves, therefore, under the mighty hand of God so that at the proper time he may exalt you..." (1Peter 5:6)*

44. 2CORINTHIANS 1:8, KJV
45. PHILIPPIANS 4:18
46. PHILIPPIANS 2:13, NKJV

ACKNOWLEDGING
MY TWO ABORTIONS

**PRINCIPLE:** IT IS ALWAYS MOST DIFFICULT TO ADMIT OUR DEEPEST SIN AND FOOLISHNESS.

Nothing saddens my heart more than admitting I refused to allow two of my children to live. It is only because I've been completely forgiven, and I believe they are in Heaven, that I can even mention it. But my open admission was years in the making.

I'd been a Christ-follower for nine years before I acknowledged my 1st abortion. It occurred while living for a year and a half with a girl in college that I said I loved. She got pregnant and pleaded with me to get married and have the baby. I refused. The coward I was drove her to a building in lower Manhattan in September of 1971, before the Roe vs. Wade decision that legalized abortion, and gave her $100 to vacuum away our child.

It would be a few more years before I admitted an earlier abortion with another college girlfriend. She had come to me in tears saying she was pregnant with my baby. My response? I berated her and dismissed her accusation. Years later, and before I received Jesus, I saw her in a store and asked her forgiveness. With tears streaming down her face, she forgave me. But, it would be another year before I received the forgiveness only Jesus can provide.

I don't completely understand why it took me years, even after coming to know Jesus, before I acknowledged the gravity of these abortions. Until then, I chalked them up as a "problem-solved." It seems the implication of my sin was so deep, I chose to live in denial than admit I had given "The fruit of my body for the sin of my soul..."

**No one leaves the planet without wishing they could go back in time...go back to a moment of weakness, a poor decision, words that should not have been said and actions we wish we'd never done. We're all stricken by the same affliction. It's called regret. And only God can free us from its clutches. He alone sent His Son Jesus to die for our sins; even for every mistake we've ever made.**

**SCRIPTURE** *"...one thing I do: forgetting what lies behind and straining forward to what lies ahead..." (Philippians 3:13b)*

47. MICAH 6:7

# DAY 48 GOD SPEAKING CHANGES EVERYTHING

**PRINCIPLE:** ONE CONVERSATION AND COMMISSION FROM GOD CAN TRANSFORM OUR LIVES.

For the first nine years of my Christian life I was unable to clearly discern the prophetic voice of God. I witnessed other leaders hearing Him but could never find an on-ramp for myself. Then in 1981, God clearly spoke to my heart, while I was taking a shower, that He was going use me to help others hear His voice. Though I had never heard the audible voice of God, somehow this impression was so distinct, I knew it was God. I responded in my mind, "But I know nothing about the subject." Here again His answer was clear. He was going to teach me. My lack of understanding about how to hear God's voice was my credential, not my disqualification. He wanted me to learn from scratch so that He would get all the glory.

This began a three-year journey of fasting, prayer and dissecting the New Testament; creating a seminar called "Spirit-Led Evangelism." I taught tens of thousands of people, either live or on video, how to hear God's voice. Simultaneously, I began to minister prophetically over hundreds and eventually thousands of people.

On one occasion, I was thousands of miles away from my daughters, who were in their early teens. Following a distinct impression, I called them and said, "Are you watching something on T.V. you shouldn't be?" Stunned, they said, "Yes!"

Another time, again while far away, I called my wife and asked her to give the phone to one of my daughters who was still lying in her bed waking up. I then prophesied about the struggling thoughts she was having as she lay there and prayed for her.

**I have come to the conviction that God is speaking to us, throughout our day, if we would just choose to hear Him. Jesus said, "My sheep hear my voice, and I know them, and they follow me."[48] Ask Jesus to teach you to hear His voice. It will transform your life!**

---

**SCRIPTURE** *"Long ago, at many times and in many ways, God spoke to our fathers by the prophets, but in these last days he has spoken to us by his Son..." (Hebrews 1:1–2)*

48. JOHN 10:27

# PORN'S TRYING TO KILL ME

**PRINCIPLE:** ALLOW GOD TO HEAL THE AREA IN YOUR LIFE THAT COULD DESTROY YOU.

**Do you know the area of your greatest vulnerability? You better! Because the enemy of your soul is stalking you in that very spot: the underbelly of your weakest point.**

Perhaps the most embarrassing sentence I could ever say is, "I'm attracted to porn!" Sad, but true! Not that I ever watch it. I don't.

But, unfortunately, I am drawn to it just the same. Because I know it would kill my spiritual life, destroy my marriage, crush my children, and end my public ministry, I keep watch over it as if it were the plague. Because it is! **I hate sin. I fight for my spiritual life every day. I cling to Jesus as my Lord and God.**

I have guards on all media. But, even with that, one unsuspecting day, the enemy attacked me in this vulnerable part of my life. I had accepted a new person as a friend on Facebook. Before doing this I always examine their Facebook page to see if they're safe and then I accept the invitation. One woman seemed safe and so I accepted her friend request. When I clicked on an email she sent me alerting me to a new Facebook post, I was bombarded with full-on pornography. I clicked off immediately, but realized once again: **if my enemy can't get me to give up, he'll try and get me to give in.**

The Bible says, "Be sober-minded; be watchful. Your adversary the devil prowls around like a roaring lion, seeking someone to devour."[49] God's Word challenges us to..."Resist the devil and he will flee."[50]

**Unless the pleasure we find in God is greater than the pleasure we find in sin, we will succumb to the evils of Earth rather than obtain the holiness of Heaven.**

**If we refuse to allow the Creator of the Universe to fascinate us, we will chase after pleasure imposters.**

**SCRIPTURE** *"...so that Satan will not outsmart us. For we are familiar with his evil schemes." (2Corinthians 2:11, NLT) "In Your presence is fullness of joy. At Your right hand are pleasures forevermore." (Psalm 16:11b, NKJV)*

49. 1PETER 5:8
50. JAMES 4:7

GOING AGAINST
THE WIND SAVED THEM

**PRINCIPLE:** WE MUST BE WILLING TO GO AGAINST THE
WIND IN ORDER TO FIND OUR WAY HOME.

A pastor friend of mine used to live in the Yukon Territory, one of the northern-most provinces of Canada. One winter day he went hunting on snowmobiles with a couple of natives. Hours into their journey a violent storm came upon them. After a long period of fighting the snow, their lead guide gestured for the three of them to stop and talk. With howling winds and piercing snow buffeting them, they huddled together. The guide confessed, "I think we're lost. I've grown up here my whole life, and I've never seen this rise in the terrain before." At those words the pastor's heart sank. Their guide was renowned. For him to be lost in a blinding snowstorm was terrifying and unexpected. After a few moments of reflection, the pastor sheepishly said, "We need to pray."

**Bowing their heads in desperation, they asked the Lord for His mercy and guidance.**

Following an emotional prayer, one of them spoke up, "I believe we've been going in the wrong direction. Because of the intensity of the storm, we've been going with the wind. What we need to do now is drive directly into the wind and snow." For a few moments after this unorthodox declaration they remained silent. Either this radical recommendation was a Word of Knowledge, or it would lead them to certain death. After another desperate prayer, they decided to receive the counsel. Though the wind and snow continued to batter them, they drove directly into the storm and eventually made it safely home.

What had saved their lives? In addition to the marvelous grace of God, they had been willing to do what hurt the most: face their fears and drive directly into the unknown. **We only change when our willingness to accept God-allowed pain exceeds our fears. At times, we will all suffer a sharp painful disillusionment before we fully surrender. Even Jesus had to endure a painful crucifixion before He could say, "It is finished!"**[51]

**SCRIPTURE** *"We are pressed on every side by troubles, but we are not crushed. We are perplexed, but not driven to despair. We are hunted down, but never abandoned by God. We get knocked down, but we are not destroyed. Through suffering, our bodies continue to share in the death of Jesus so that the life of Jesus may also be seen in our bodies." (2Corinthians 4:8–10, NLT)*

51. JOHN 19:30

# GIVING AWAY OUR ONLY CAR

**PRINCIPLE:** GOD ASKS US TO GIVE WHAT WE THINK WE NEED; IN ORDER TO RECEIVE WHAT WE REALLY NEED.

I was once speaking at a family camp in Canada when a call "to give" came over the meetings. God prompted me to give away our only car. I called my wife and asked her to pray about doing this. She called the next day and agreed. As God would have it, someone else then gave us a car. The test was passed and our need was met.

**God's a total giver! Does He have to give? Absolutely not! He owns everything!**

The Bible says, "The earth is the Lord's, and everything in it. The world and all its people belong to Him."[52] God doesn't want to make your life a "have to;" He delights in making it a glorious "get to." Every blessing we have is because of His grace. "Every good gift and every perfect gift is from above, and comes down from the Father of lights..."[53]

**God's looking for people who are willing to distribute His products: His love, His joy, His peace, His forgiveness, and His kindness.**
He'll bless anyone who's willing to stay unattached to the things He gives them. Many times, He wants us just to be intermediaries, "flowing rivers of blessing," not "stagnant pools of entitlement."

You can be a bird and not fly. You can be a fish and not swim. You can be married and not love your spouse. But why would you want to live beneath your potential? I choose to obey God and believe that I get to do the things He's called me to. I get to receive the love of my Creator. I get to follow His majestic plan for my life. I get to love others as He has loved me. I get to worship Him with all of my heart, soul and strength.

**Don't make following Jesus a miserable "have to." Make it a marvelous "get to."**

**SCRIPTURE** *"...give, and it will be given to you. Good measure, pressed down, shaken together, running over, will be put into your lap. For with the measure you use it will be measured back to you." (Luke 6:38)*

52. PSALM 24:1, NLT
53. JAMES 1:17, NKJV

# SOLICITING A PROSTITUTE IN AMSTERDAM

**PRINCIPLE:** AT TIMES, WE MUST DO THE RIDICULOUS IN ORDER TO SEE THE MIRACULOUS.

In 1983, I attended a Billy Graham conference with 5,000 evangelists from around the world, staying in a hostel in the "red light" district. Every night, another evangelist and I passed by a particular prostitute who'd try and solicit us. One night, we sensed the Holy Spirit was encouraging us to accept her invitation, in order to share the gospel. During our 30 minutes talking with her, we found out that she had deep wounds from being rejected by a boyfriend. She cried and we prayed with her. A powerful, eternal seed had been planted.

Why doesn't God punish evil people, swiftly and justly? Why are they allowed to hurt and destroy? The question can best be answered when we consider an evil person we each personally know. Someone we've grown up with. We've seen not just their actions, but know intimately their motives. Someone like...us! I am most familiar with an evil person called "me." The Bible says, "...for all have sinned and fall short of the glory of God."[54]

**How many of you would like God to punish you quickly? Frankly, when it comes to me, I'm more a fan of mercy than judgment.** As the Bible teaches, "God, who is rich in mercy, because of His great love with which He loved us, even when we were dead in trespasses, made us alive together with Christ..."[55]

The enemy of our soul has always offered counterfeit fulfillment. **Most people expend huge amounts of time, energy, and money staying current on the temporary, illusive pleasures of life, while missing out on the tangible, eternal pleasures of God in the process. God has the answer for every inferior pleasure. As a matter of fact, God is the answer!** Knowing the God who created pleasure is the only way to experience the real thing, and not the counterfeit. Accept no substitutes for a genuine, life-long relationship with your Creator. It's the only way to a guilt-free, pleasure-filled life. The Bible says, "You will show me the path of life; in Your presence is fullness of joy; at Your right hand are pleasures forevermore."[56]

**SCRIPTURE** *"So they went and entered the house of a prostitute named Rahab and stayed there." (Joshua 2:1b)*

54. ROMANS 3:23, NKJV
55. EPHESIANS 2:4–5, NKJV
56. PSALM 16:11, NKJV

# AFRAID OF
THE DARK

**PRINCIPLE:** OUR FEARS ONLY LEAVE US WHEN WE FACE THEM.

Even though my father had his picture on the front page of the New York Times when he died, he was still afraid of the dark, would sleep with a light on, and once even had his barber spend the night due to fear.

**I grew up with a fear of the dark as well but conquered it by confronting it.**

I was speaking in Louisiana, a place that has more bugs and critters than anywhere in America. Listening to the sheer volume of noise emanating from their forests gave me the chills. The parsonage at the church I was speaking at had a lot of dark, mysterious rooms. One night, I was up praying and the Holy Spirit led me to go room to room, with all of the lights out, and put my hands in places no hands should go: under beds, on closet shelves. I put them there and kept them there until my heart was settled and the fears were vanquished.

**Every virtue stands on the shoulders of courage.** Without courage we will not allow the God of love to captivate our hearts, the Prince of Peace to be our rest, and the joy of the Lord to be our strength. **Without courage we will give up too soon, show up too late, and believe for too little. Bowing to fear is the least safe thing we can do.**

**At times, being brave means being courageous five minutes longer than those around us.** Though we will all fight weariness, we must hold fast to the call of God on our lives, and the promises of God we have each been given.

**Courage is best seen in a humble Man walking up a hill carrying a cross.**

---

**SCRIPTURE** *"...for God gave us a spirit not of fear but of power and love and self-control." (2Timothy 1:7)*

# THE PROPHETIC
## *1985–1999* YEARS

# THE PROPHETIC
*1985–1999* YEARS

WITH BEAUTIFUL SUZIE!

MOTHER, THE STATELY MATRIARCH

MOTHER AND SOME OF HER GRANDCHILDREN

PREACHING AS AN EVANGELIST IN THE 1980'S    PREACHING AS BRAVEHEART

SUZIE & OUR GIRLS IN 1991

# MOJAVE DESERT MIRACLE

**PRINCIPLE:** SEEDS OF HOPE WE PLANT IN OTHER PEOPLE WILL REAP MIRACLES.

**There was a man who, for years, would call me in the middle of the night from some chamber of hell.** Sometimes the phone would ring, and I would say 'Hello," but there would be no response. Knowing it was him I would say, "Bruce?" and he would share a few words describing the emotional, drug-induced pit he was in. I would pray and hang up saddened over his tragic, broken life.

One day, Bruce had come to such a desperate place he was contemplating ending his life. Hitchhiking in the Mojave Desert, in the middle of nowhere, he shot up a fleeting prayer. **"God, if you can still help me, send someone to take me to Francis."** A few minutes later a car pulled up, and a man named Dennis offered him a ride. In their conversation, Bruce said he wanted to go to South Lake Tahoe. Dennis responded with, "Hey, I've got a good friend there—Francis Anfuso." Bruce was shocked. God had answered the most outrageous of prayers. But Dennis wasn't just an average person. He was an anointed man of God who then spent hours driving and ministering powerfully to Bruce.

**All of us want a 2nd chance. Actually, we all need a 2nd chance. And the best news is: God wants to give it to us.** Another opportunity to learn how to live—to be "Born Again," to stop making ourselves the center of the universe—because, we're not. To stop insisting on getting our expectations fulfilled, when God has a much better plan. It will take faith to receive it and patience to wait for it. We'll need to swat away the flies of disappointment and discouragement. But, in the end, we'll look back and see God was always worth waiting for.

**Today, invite the "God of 2nd Chances" to be the Lord of your life. Jesus said, "I tell you the truth; unless you are born again, you cannot see the Kingdom of God."**[57]

**SCRIPTURE** *"Now an angel of the Lord said to Philip, 'Rise and go toward the south to the road that goes down from Jerusalem to Gaza.' This is a desert place." (Acts 8:26)*

57. JOHN 3:3, NLT

# ALL THE TIMES I'VE MISSED GOD

**PRINCIPLE:** OUR HEARTS BREAK WHEN WE THINK ABOUT THE TIMES WE'VE FOOLISHLY MISSED GOD.

**Looking back over my life, I've learned far more from my failures than my successes. We reflect little after a home run, but striking out is always a wakeup call.**

One particular situation that illustrates this happened when I was living in South Lake Tahoe. I had spent the day with Suzie and my young daughters relaxing by a mountain stream. It was a 15-minute hike from our parked car. Arriving back at the car, I realized, much to my dismay, that I had left a nice pair of sunglasses by the stream. After running back and finding them, on my return to the car I passed a man sitting on log looking emotionally devastated. Though my heart tugged to stop and talk with him, I didn't.

**Sadly, I was too upset over having to go back for the sunglasses to care for someone in need.**

**He had not been there just minutes before. Yet, now I firmly believe he was providentially placed directly in my path. I can't count the number of times I've been deeply saddened thinking about him. The phantom man has been the fuel for hundreds of other divine appointments I have, thank God, not missed.**

We shouldn't be surprised when God interrupts us. Often times, it's the only way He can get our attention. In my youth, I would stay up late to seek the Lord. As I've gotten older, I get up early, every morning, to pray and get into the Word while listening to worship music. This uninterrupted time alone with the Lord is vital for me. In these moments, I hear His voice and know His direction for my life and those I am called to lead. Most of us are leading someone, or in time we will be. So, it's vitally important that we learn to let God lead us. And that will usually begin with divine interruptions.

**Today, will you let God interrupt you? It will certainly be worth your while.**

---

**SCRIPTURE** *"...be ready in season and out of season; reprove, rebuke, and exhort, with complete patience and teaching." (2Timothy 4:2)*

# OBSCENE PHONE CALL WITH MY MOTHER-IN-LAW

**PRINCIPLE:** GOD CAN USE THE MOST BIZARRE SITUATIONS TO REACH SOMEONE LOST.

I had the privilege of leading Suzie's mother to Jesus, after she had been backslidden for 50 years. A few weeks later, Suzie and I were sitting around her kitchen table, having joined hands and about to pray, when the phone rang. Answering it, she held the phone to her chest and with a horrified look gasped, "It's an obscene phone call!" Grabbing the phone, I heard a man yelling profanities. Responding primarily on instinct, I yelled back, "I know why you're calling! You're a lonely, miserable person. But, God had you call this number because He wants to set you free..."

This continued on for about a minute, with both of us yelling. When I realized I couldn't hear him anymore, I blurted out, "Well? What do you think?" A few seconds later, he said in a normal voice. "I think you're right!" This began a 15-minute discussion. He was a bored, 19-year old being stupid. I told him I forgave him for what he did and even scheduled a meeting to talk more. Though he didn't show up, I knew a seed of love had been planted.

We all fall and fail! But, our failing, and the despair it generates, can't compare with the depth of despair the devil faces every day. He knows deep down, his efforts to destroy us will only end in absolute failure. **Our failing is our sad beginning! His failing will be his tragic end! Our failing creates the plot and tension that eventually leads to our rescue, and one of the great joys in life: realizing that all the devil meant for evil has turned out for God's glory and my good.**

**He who laughs last, laughs best! That Person would be God, and those who belong to Him. Never forget, the God who created laughter, loves to laugh, and if we surrender our lives to Him, we will laugh and rejoice around His throne forever.**

**SCRIPTURE** *"...be ready in season and out of season; reprove, rebuke, and exhort, with complete patience and teaching." (2Timothy 4:2)*

# THE SILLIEST THING I EVER DID

**PRINCIPLE:** OBEYING THE HOLY SPIRIT WILL, AT TIMES, SEEM ABSOLUTELY FOOLISH.

While ministering in the Gifts of the Spirit over the years, the Holy Spirit led me to, at times, do things that were peculiar, even outlandish. Not that Jesus ever put mud in a blind man's eyes,[58] Peter stepped out of a boat to walk on water,[59] or Paul went to Jerusalem after he was told and believed that prison and hardships were waiting for him.[60] Night after night, I would minister over dozens and dozens of people. I once prophesied over a woman with a severe spinal malformation. All I said was, "Pop! Pop! Pop! Pop! Pop! Pop! Pop!" What? To say the least, I felt foolish. Who was I, "Sugar Pops Pete?"

A couple of years went by, and I ran into her again. She came running up so excited to see me and shared that she had gone to a doctor and found out that she had seven deformed vertebrae in her back. My prophetic word, with seven distinct "Pops", had profoundly encouraged her that one day she would hear that sound and be healed. **God had given her something priceless...HOPE!**

**Whoever has the most hope...wins!** We all wonder why certain things happen; some good, and some bad. Is anyone behind the wheel of our lives? Is anyone guiding and watching over our souls? The truth is, there are no accidental sparrows or snowflakes and no coincidental moments or mountains to climb. All things are carefully choreographed by the Great Dancer in the Sky, the Glorious God who right now is contemplating every molecule in the universe; none more special than the ones that make up His sons and daughters.

**We each are given a daily opportunity to have as much hope as God does.** That is why the psalmist wrote, "Why am I discouraged? Why is my heart so sad? I will put my hope in God! I will praise Him again— my Savior and my God!"[61] **Never forget: hope is eternal and being freely offered to you, each and every day!**

**SCRIPTURE** *'For the foolishness of God is wiser than men, and the weakness of God is stronger than men." (1Corinthians 1:25)*

58. JOHN 9:6
59. MATTHEW 14:29
60. ACTS 20:23
61. PSALM 43:5, NLT

**PRINCIPLE:** BETTER TO DIE TRYING, THAN TO LIVE UNWILLING TO DO THE RIGHT THING.

When my family and I lived in South Lake Tahoe in the 1980's, I had an experience that still gives me chills. Lake Tahoe is a majestic alpine lake that is extremely cold and deep. One year, our church family held a picnic on the shores of the lake. I was standing on the shoreline with a couple of close friends when we realized a distant speck on the horizon was the couple's eight-year old daughter, Kathryn. She was on a raft being pulled out across the frigid lake by the wind, with absolutely no one around her.

The father was an overweight man and was fully clothed. The mother was an athletic woman who had a bathing suit on underneath sweats. Without saying a word, the mom slipped her sweats off and dove into the freezing lake. She was, as they say in poker, "All in!"

My frantic mind raced. "If I go in, what if I die?" The day before two capsized boaters had drowned of hypothermia in this glacial lake. Yet all of these thoughts were countered by my final conclusion: "I will never be able to live with myself if I don't do something! If the mother was willing to die for her child, I had to be as well." I took off my sweatshirt and went into the freezing water. It felt like diving into fire. A good swimmer, yet nearly 40 years old, I quickly tired. Soon, I no longer felt like a rescuer—I was swimming to survive. My body was exhausted and freezing. It is still a miracle that we made it to her raft and back.

**The mother told me later, 'If you had not joined me, I would not have made it back!" What provokes me even now was how perilously close I came to doing nothing. The mother's commitment to save her child still inspires me, far more than my own, and reminds me yet again of the selfless sacrifice Jesus made for each of us.**

**SCRIPTURE** *"Then Elijah stood in front of them and said, 'How much longer will you waver, hobbling between two opinions? If the LORD is God, follow him! But if Baal is God, then follow him!' But the people were completely silent." (1Kings 18:21)*

# LEADING A WHOLE RESTAURANT IN PRAYER

**PRINCIPLE:** YOU MIGHT BE SURPRISED HOW OBEYING GOD BRINGS EXTRAORDINARY RESULTS.

I was once in a crowded restaurant on a Sunday after church with a pastor friend when the Lord prompted me to invite the entire restaurant to pray. I stood up with a big smile and said to the 50 people who could hear me, "Could I have your attention please?" The busy room went completely silent in about 10 seconds. I continued, "You know, we're having such a wonderful time here with family and friends in this great restaurant, why don't we just take a moment and thank God for this beautiful day?"

I then bowed my head and offered a brief, uplifting prayer before sitting down. What happened next was even more surprising. The pastor I was with said, "You know, I never would have thought what you just did would have been so peaceable, but it was." Throughout the meal, people began to come over and thank me; even waitresses. My fear of man wasn't able to control me, and the ACLU didn't have time to stop me. God had His way in that glorious day!

**It's funny, how just obeying God at times is the best thing we can do.**

What do people see in us? The Bible says, "...God made two great lights, the sun and the moon..."[62] Jesus, like the sun, is the greater light that doesn't reflect; He imparts. On the other hand, we are the lesser light; the moon. We merely reflect the light of the sun. We have no light outside of the Holy Spirit within us! Without God, we reflect and impart nothing of eternal value. Yet, Jesus encourages us, "You are the light of the world." [63]

**If Jesus is our Lord, then we are called to be a light in a world lost in darkness. As moons, we can only reflect the light of the sun, Jesus.**

**In a world full of darkness, we are even brighter than distant suns. We may be the only light people ever see.**

---

**SCRIPTURE** *"...be ready in season and out of season; reprove, rebuke, and exhort, with complete patience and teaching." (2Timothy 4:2)*

62. GENESIS 1:16A, NLT
63. MATTHEW 5:14, NLT

# WRONG PLANE LEADS TO CRUSHING LOSS

**PRINCIPLE:** HOW WE RESPOND TO SETBACKS WILL DETERMINE HOW SUCCESSFUL WE ARE.

Throughout the 1980's I had the privilege of speaking at the largest Christian Festival in America. 30,000 people gathered for music and teaching. It was always marvelous! One year, I was invited to speak on the main stage on Friday night after Michael W. Smith, who was at the height of his musical career. It was a privilege, and I did well. The next year I was invited back to do the same thing. Unfortunately, I made the miscalculation of thinking I could fly into a closer airport. It was a big mistake. The new airport was actually much further away, and by the time I landed, and calculated the driving distance, there was no possibility of arriving on time. A crushing blow and one I could not remedy. I sincerely asked the forgiveness of those in charge for my error in judgment, and of course received it, but a grand opportunity was missed.

All I had left was my response. And from the moment I realized my error, I did my best to respond in a godly way in front of my observing wife, children and a close friend. My heart was hurting, but this was now a test of my character, and I did not want to fail.

Playwright David Mamet writes, "...most people lost in the wilds...die of shame... 'What did I do wrong? How could I have gotten myself into this?' And so they sit there and they...die. Because they didn't do the one thing that would save their lives."

**The Bible says we are all lost, but we don't have to die of shame if we look "...to Jesus the author and finisher of our faith; who for the joy that was set before him endured the cross, despising the shame, and is set down at the right hand of the throne of God."**[64] He despised the shame of becoming sin for us because He knew it would lead to the rescue of all humanity; who would turn from sin to Him. The greatest shame is not wholeheartedly believing this marvelous truth.

---

**SCRIPTURE** *"Beloved, do not be surprised at the fiery trial when it comes upon you to test you, as though something strange were happening to you." (1Peter 4:12)*

64. HEBREWS 12:2

# MISSPEAKING AT AN ABORTION DEBATE

---

**PRINCIPLE:** OUR HUMILIATION CAN WORK FOR OUR GOOD, IF WE CHOOSE TO RESPOND WELL.

---

In the late 1980's, I was a leader in the pro-life movement in South Lake Tahoe. A debate was held in our city between Phyllis Schlafly, a notable constitutional lawyer, and Sarah Weddington, the lawyer who successfully presented the infamous Roe vs. Wade case, legalizing abortion, before the U.S. Supreme Court. One thousand people, mostly pro-abortion, were packed in a ballroom. The room was tense, with the boisterous audience chiding Schlafly and cheering Weddington.

At one point I stood up to share. There was an audible sigh from the pro-life folks who were excited that someone they respected was at last going to ask a question. Sadly, when I spoke, my words were not effective, and I even misspoke during my description of a woman's pregnancy. The biased audience laughed and cheered as Weddington twisted my words and further humiliated me. **It was a sad day and one I would not soon forget.**

Do you feel like a failure? All of us will, at times, see ourselves in this way. But there's an absolute cure: knowing the One who died to make us a success—not in the eyes of the world, nor even in our own eyes, but in His eyes—the eyes of the only Person who knows what's best for us. **I choose to see my life from God's perspective—the finished product; the person He intended me to be.**

When Adam and Eve sinned, God first said to them, "Where are you?" not "What have you done?" **This is another clear indication that God's far more concerned about our relationship with Him than anything bad we've done. He's first a Dad who wants to help and protect.** That's why the Bible says, "The LORD keeps you from all harm and watches over your life." **Since we all sin, it's vital that we know when we blow it, we can run to God and not away from Him.**

**Turn yourself in! Don't wait to be caught!**
**No one cares more for you than Jesus.**

---

**SCRIPTURE** *"I am he who blots out your transgressions for my own sake, and I will not remember your sins." (Isaiah 43:25) "For I will forgive their iniquity, and I will remember their sin no more." (Jeremiah 31:34)*

65. PSALM 121:7, NLT

# CHASING DOWN A PURSE SNATCHER

**PRINCIPLE:** THE BIGGEST HYPOCRITE I CAN EVER IMPACT IS... MYSELF.

When I was in my early 40's, after speaking at a church in Southern California, my family and I were packing our car to leave a hotel. Piercing the quiet of the morning, I heard someone yell, "Stop him! He stole her purse!" Fifty feet away, a thief ran by with a purse in his hand, and two men chasing him. Instinctively, I started to run as well.

Because the chase had begun a few blocks away at an outdoor restaurant, I and another man were fresh enough to catch the thief. While detaining him on his back on the ground, and waiting for the police to arrive, I thought it would be a great opportunity to speak about Jesus. Still breathing heavily, with a crowd gathering and him lying on the ground, we locked eyes and I whispered; "I know God brought me to you because I'm a Christian."

**Immediately, his eyes got wide and he shot back, "I'm a Christian too!" WHAT! It was the last thing I expected him to say!**

**But, it brought to light perhaps life's greatest challenge. Am I representing Jesus in a way that does justice to who He is and the marvelous work He's done in my life?**

People say, "The church has too many hypocrites!" It's true! The planet's packed with hypocrites and some of them are in churches. A hypocrite is someone who's not always honest; who says one thing and then does another. Do you feel like you have ever fit this definition? I know I have! Yet, I am the only person, besides God, who really knows how big of a hypocrite I am. And the ultimate judge of my hypocrisy is God Himself. Paul the Apostle wrote, "He who judges me is the Lord. Therefore, judge nothing before the time, until the Lord comes, who will both bring to light the hidden things of darkness and reveal the counsels of the hearts. Then each one's praise will come from God."

**If you want to see a decrease in hypocrisy in the church, work on your own heart.**

**SCRIPTURE** *Jesus said, "Not everyone who says to me, 'Lord, Lord,' will enter the kingdom of heaven, but the one who does the will of my Father who is in heaven." (Matthew 7:21)*

66. 1CORINTHIANS 4:4B-5, NKJV

GIVING GOD 100% PROFIT
FROM OUR FIRST HOME

**PRINCIPLE:** FAITH AND OBEDIENCE ARE THE ONLY APPROPRIATE
RESPONSE TO A GOD WHO LONGS TO BLESS YOU.

When my wife and I sold our first home in South Lake Tahoe, we made the decision to sow 100% of our equity, $50,000, to the Lord. We placed it in the ministry we were a part of, and then rented for the next eight years. It was a decision, I believe, that put us in a position for our next home to be sold, in 2005, for a $270,000 profit.

**The key, as always, was obedience!**

As a young Christian, I had a job cleaning a restaurant's kitchen. No matter how spotless I made it, it would be a mess the next day. One day as I was mopping my way out, I caught a strand of the mop on the leg of a dishwasher. Though I initially thought, "I'll get it tomorrow." God sent me back 15 minutes after leaving the kitchen to pick it up. Now, over forty years later, I'm still obeying and seeing the value of little things.

**We can spend our lives waiting to see a tree, when God wants us to first see a seed. The abundance of a garden starts with the tiniest sprout. If we can't see the value of the seed, we'll never reap its abundance.** The Bible says, "Do not despise these small beginnings, for the LORD rejoices to see the work begin."

Though many American Christians are supernaturally, and even naturally "rich," they have a "poverty mindset." A person with a poverty mindset is afraid he won't have enough if he gives. What does it make him do? It makes him close up. And as soon as God's call comes to give, if we have a poverty mindset, our response will be, "I don't have enough to give. I can't afford it." **If God wants to make you a river of His blessing, why should you remain a stagnant pool of poverty? The "poverty mindset" has to be broken in us if we are going to ever do His will on Earth. Don't look at your career or checkbook as your source, when the truth is God is the source and reward for everything He'll ever ask you to do.**

**SCRIPTURE** *"I am he who blots out your transgressions for my own sake, and I will not remember your sins." (Isaiah 43:25) "For I will forgive their iniquity, and I will remember their sin no more." (Jeremiah 31:34)*

67. ZECHARIAH 4:10, NLT

# DAY 64 RENDEZVOUS IN THE UTTER-MOST PART OF THE EARTH

1990

**PRINCIPLE:** ONE OF THE GREAT JOYS IN LIFE IS
SEEING GOD MOVE AFTER WE'VE GIVEN UP.

In 1990, when Suzie, our daughters and I toured New Zealand, the last concert on the nine-city tour was in Invercargill, New Zealand, the southernmost city in that island nation. As you enter the city there is a sign that reads: "Welcome to Invercargill, New Zealand – The Uttermost Part of the Earth." Apparently, Invercargill is the furthest city from Jerusalem on Earth. It was, to say the least, a peculiar sign, and it made a distinct impression. The expression "uttermost part of the earth" is taken from Acts 1:8 in the King James Version of the Bible, "But ye shall receive power, after that the Holy Ghost is come upon you: and ye shall be witnesses unto me both in Jerusalem, and in all Judaea, and in Samaria, and unto the **uttermost part of the earth."**

The complete impact of the sign did not hit me until a few days later, when we were about to fly out of the country from Invercargill. I had been working on an intense creative project, and was saddened that I had not been able to rendezvous with a long-time friend and advisor, Winkie Pratney. At that time, Winkie and his family would spend half the year living in the U.S. and the other half in his hometown of Auckland. We had been with them in both places and had looked forward to being together again. But it was not to be.

As we were sitting on the 30-seater plane, loading passengers, I was reflecting on the fact that I had missed seeing Winkie. How sad! As the thought crossed my mind, Winkie walked on the plane. Neither of us knew where the other was on Earth, but God did. We then spent the next two hours, as we flew to Auckland, catching up on our personal lives and discussing the project. His advice, as always, was just what I needed. I was amazed by the sovereignty of God in this situation. **As I reflected on it, God spoke to my heart, "I can meet your needs from the uttermost parts of the earth."**

**God has proven Himself more than faithful to me. He promises to do the same for you.**

---

**SCRIPTURE** *"Look at the birds of the air: they neither sow nor reap nor gather into barns, and yet your heavenly Father feeds them. Are you not of more value than they?" (Matthew 6:26)*

---

**PRINCIPLE:**   GOD CAN FIND WILLING HEARTS TO DO FOR US
WHAT WE CANNOT.

---

A woman once approached me after a church service where I had just ministered, wanting to give my wife, who was not with me, a ring. Initially, I walked away saying I couldn't accept it, but she pursued; asking, "What is her ring size?" I didn't have a clue, but blurted out her shoe size, "Five." She smiled, and with tears in her eyes, took a beautiful diamond ring off her finger saying, "This is for your wife. God wants her to know how much He loves her." After a discussion with the pastor of the church, I accepted it.

When I gave it to Suzie, she put it on without examining it, pressing the back of the ring thinking it was costume jewelry. But God had given something special to Suzie, and it spoke to her in ways only she understood.

Why did God direct this stranger to give so extravagantly? I have to assume it was because of exactly what she said, "God wants her to know how much He loves her." We weren't chasing after anything, but we were open to discern and receive all God had for us.

Why are so many of us dissatisfied? Is it perhaps because the world system wants us to be discontent? You'll never hear a commercial say, "You've got to be content with what you have. Our product won't give you contentment. Save your money and buy only what you really need."

**Trying to find contentment by buying things is like eating pretzels to quench your thirst. The more you buy, the more you want: even if you can't afford that kind of house, that kind of car, or those clothes. Make it look like you can.**

**The truth is that there's nothing wrong with having nice things; if it's God's will for your life, if they don't have you, and if you can afford them. Paul wrote, "I have learned to be content with whatever I have."**[68]

---

**SCRIPTURE** *"Now to him who is able to do far more abundantly than all that we ask or think, according to the power at work within us…" (Ephesians 3:20)*

68. PHILIPPIANS 4:11, NRSV

# MIDNIGHT ENCOUNTER WITH A GREAT DANE

**PRINCIPLE:** OUR GREATEST VICTORIES OCCUR WHEN WE HAVE NO ONE TO RESCUE US BUT GOD.

I used to go for walks at night, to walk and pray. One night, around midnight, I was strolling in my neighborhood and, all of a sudden, a man opened his front door to let his dog, a massive Great Dane, out. Immediately, this dog, as big as a horse, ran out, leapt over a hedge and made a beeline for me. It happened so quickly all I could do was freeze. He then jumped up, put his giant paws on my shoulders, and without missing a beat licked my face, from chin to forehead. Then, just as quickly, he turned around, did his thing on the ground and went back into his house.

It was unbelievable! But, as I reflect on it now, there's probably no better example of the Bible verse that says, "Stand still and see the salvation of God." [69]

All of us are looking for something you would think wouldn't be that hard to find. But it is! It's called REST! The Bible says, "...there is a special rest still waiting for the people of God. For all who have entered into God's rest have rested from their labors, just as God did after creating the world."[70]

**Rest! It comes from only one source—God.
And He longs to give it to each of us.**

Everything God does is holy. So, when the Bible says, "God blessed the seventh day and declared it holy, because it was the day when He rested from His work of creation,"[71] **God made resting a holy act!**

**Rest is learning to silence your soul completely; becoming utterly still, so desperately quiet inside, that at last your eyes cease their obsession with self and are firmly fixed upon God. God wants to spend time and eternity with you...to teach you how to rest in Him. It's why you were created. Rest in God!**

**SCRIPTURE** *"Look at the birds of the air: they neither sow nor reap nor gather into barns, and yet your heavenly Father feeds them. Are you not of more value than they?" (Matthew 6:26)*

69. EXODUS 14:13
70. HEBREWS 4:9–10, NLT
71. GENESIS 2:3

# PROTECTED WHEN CONFRONTED BY L.A. GANG

**PRINCIPLE:** GOD PROTECTS US EVEN WHEN WE CAN'T PROTECT OURSELVES.

When my wife and I lived in Los Angeles and our twin daughters were in Junior High, we drove them to a slumber party late one night in a very rough part of town. Arriving at 11 PM, on a poorly lit, deserted street, we decided to survey our surroundings before exiting the car. In my rear view mirror, I could see five silhouettes fanned out across the middle of the street. They looked questionable, even ominous. Who were they, and why were they walking so slowly, five feet apart toward our vehicle?

I told my wife and daughters to stay in the car. The five men came directly behind us, with the largest man standing five feet behind our car with his arms folded. He just stood there with his face in the shadows. After a minute, I said to my wife, "I'm going to get out and talk with him." Trying my driver's side door, it wouldn't open. I unlocked it over and over again, but nothing worked. After much clicking, I could see him gesture disgustedly toward our car and then proceed back in formation and continue walking.

The entire event was beyond peculiar, but got even more bizarre when a friend and I removed the door only to find the mechanics of the door had just disconnected. And there was no physical way for the mechanism to detach. **It had been a miracle! To say the least, it called into question my decision to exit the car. Something terrible could have transpired to my family and me, and God had protected us.**

**It is vitally important that I see my struggles as a test and not a threat. Greater is he who is in me than anything that could assault me. Considering the tests of Earth as threats to my well-being ultimately turns my life into a fear-based experience rather than a faith-filled opportunity, perfectly crafted for my good.**

**No one can force me to bow to fear and unbelief. The enemy cannot intimidate me, unless I allow him to. I must choose to reverently bow, each and every day, to the Holy Spirit and His protective will for my life. The Bible says, "...for in Him we live and move and have our being..."**

**SCRIPTURE** *"My Savior, You save me from violence. I will call upon the Lord, who is worthy to be praised; so shall I be saved from my enemies." (2Samuel 22:3–4)*

BEFRIENDING A FAMILY WHO
LOST FATHER AND SON

**PRINCIPLE:** GOD BRINGS PEOPLE INTO OUR LIVES
FOR BOTH THEIR GOOD AND OUR GOOD.

I have found that there are times in life when God draws us into impossible situations and commissions us to step into the unknown. I had one such experience with a family I didn't know who went through an inconceivable loss. A woman in our church named Kathy had her father and only brother killed when their small plane crashed. This left her mother Jan, a widow, and Kathy and her sister, Chy, heartbroken. I remember the exact spot I was in when I heard the news. My heart was pierced and I knew I had to reach out and help them in any way I could. This led to many years of a close friendship with my wife and I undergirding the family.

The fact that we feel completely incapable of meeting the needs of others should never paralyze us from reaching out and doing what we can. Yes, our planting and watering are nothing without God's life-giving increase, but they are the seed God uses to bring forth a harvest. Don't despise the seed faith he gives you. It will always be enough to start.

Have you ever asked yourself, "What on Earth do I want to be?" It's an important question and will determine what you and I will be in eternity. I've thought a lot about it, and **as for me, I want to be like Jesus! He is the person who has blessed my life the most. He is the One who loves me the most; and died in my place.**

**I want my person and character to represent Jesus so well that when people see me they feel like they're looking into the face of Jesus. If I forget who I am created to be, I'll always wind up becoming some-one less than God intended. And that would be a tragic mistake I don't want to make. The Bible says, "In him we live and move and have our being."[73]**

SCRIPTURE *"Then a despised Samaritan came along, and when he saw the man, he felt compassion for him. Going over to him, the Samaritan soothed his wounds with olive oil and wine and bandaged them. Then he put the man on his own donkey and took him to an inn, where he took care of him." (Luke 10:33-34, NLT)*

73. EXODUS 14:13

# MIRACLE IN THE FIRST OPENLY ATHEISTIC NATION

**PRINCIPLE:** AT THE POINT YOU FEEL THE ENEMY HAS WON... LOOK AND PRAY AGAIN.

**God is never intimidated, and He never shows up too late. Never!**

My twin brother, Joseph, was always an incredible writer. Even his postcards from far-flung places were captivating. I remember sitting around with members of my family reading them aloud and thinking, "Wow, what a description!"

Joseph tells the story of his journey to Albania in 1994, a nation that had proudly declared itself, "the world's first atheist state." He went with a uniquely prophetic man named Jim Goll. Growing up on a remote Missouri farm with few friends, Jim developed a regular communication with Jesus as a young child. Joseph knew that God frequently used Jim, as he put it, "as an agent of SerenDestiny."

The Albanian landscape was as barren as many of its people, with "...reminders of a troubled past: empty factories, thousands of dome-shaped bunkers, and valleys carpeted with tall concrete columns topped by sharp iron spikes. They were supposed to impale paratroopers'"[74] their paranoid leader thought would come, but never did.

One night in a crowded theater, where the atmosphere seemed more like a boxing match than a church service, the room was packed with many standing along the walls. Joseph shared for 20 minutes or so, but the audience was generally disinterested. Jim went outside to pray, and then stepped up and said, "My friend told you that God is with us in the room tonight, and I want to prove that to you. Is there a woman here named Sarai?" A woman in the back timidly raised her hand. The room got quieter. "You have a small lump on your left breast, don't you?" She nodded. You could hear a pin drop. After praying for her, a dozen additional people rushed forward to see if the living God might touch them as well. As Joseph recounts, "It was without question, one of the most extraordinary prayer meetings I have ever experienced."

**Jesus knows what it's like to lack clarity, to wonder what to do, to be down, but not out. That's why Jesus said, "...the Son can do nothing by himself. He does only what he sees the Father doing. Whatever the Father does, the Son also does."[75] He's the God of the comeback, and if you'll let Him, He'll champion your comeback as well.**

**SCRIPTURE** *"For we do not have a high priest who is unable to empathize with our weaknesses, but we have one who has been tempted in every way, just as we are—yet he did not sin." (Hebrews 4:15)*

74. EXCERPT FROM "THE BEST STORY OF YOUR LIFE" BY JOSEPH ANFUSO, PP. 86–90
75. JOHN 5:19, NLT

# MEETING PRODUCER OF FAMOUS BAND IN HOLLYWOOD

**PRINCIPLE:** YOU ARE INFINITELY MORE IMPORTANT TO GOD THAN WHATEVER YOU'RE HOPING FOR.

I walked into a dimly lit room on Sunset Boulevard in Hollywood, California. The producer of two of the most successful secular rock bands of all time, with more than 180 million albums sold, had assembled half a dozen of his creative team. He had invited me to present a 20-minute video I had produced describing a prospective multi-media youth tour. The 90-minute production was designed to reach millions of young people with a high-tech gospel message. As the video promo ended, the producer turned to me and remarked, "That was the best presentation of a project I have ever seen. I'm very interested!"

Our meeting had been set up at the request of the wealthy Christian owner of an established secular TV network. He had asked this top producer to critique the project and give recommendations. The producer's conclusion: "If he [the TV network owner] doesn't provide financing for the tour, I will." It turned out that, though this producer was not a Christian, he had a praying sister who was. Later that day he showed my video to a Warner Brothers' Vice President, and once again, it received a positive response.

I left the meeting ecstatic. Many other extraordinary contacts were made with highly capable Christians in the entertainment industry who were eager to use their gifts and resources to see this youth tour come to pass. It seemed it was all coming together.

Within weeks, the rock band producer flew to meet with a renowned Christian TV personality and myself to finalize the project. Agreements were made. Everything seemed to be on course, until a top Christian concert promoter advised the producer that there was not a large enough Christian market to make the tour viable.

**It was a marvelous concept...a brilliant presentation...but too small a market! Great miracles took place in a project God never intended to complete, because I was the project the whole time. Since God's end is always the process, He will only complete what is designed to work for my eternal good.**

**SCRIPTURE** *"...for it is God who works in you, both to will and to work for his good plea-sure." (Philippians 2:13)*

# OUR DAUGHTERS' MAIDEN MINISTRY VOYAGE

**PRINCIPLE:** LEARN TO TRUST GOD ALONE TO ACCOMPLISH HIS WILL.

When I was travelling as an evangelist, I would often bring my wife Suzie and twin daughters, Deborah and Havilah, with me. When they were just 17 years old, I sensed it was time for my daughters to step into their own ministry. So, when I was invited to a church I had ministered in before, I told the pastor my daughters had a great prophetic anointing.

At the time, though, they had never ministered publically.

Upon arriving at the church, my daughters saw advertisements for the first time saying they were scheduled to minister that night to the youth group. They were, to say the least, upset with me. But, facing the inevitable, they went up on a mountain outside the city and kneeling down with their Bibles, asked God to help them.

That night, after I had ministered in the adult meeting, my wife and I waited patiently for our daughters to be dropped off. Hour after hour passed, until, at 2 A.M., they came in elated that God had used them so mightily, even in their weakness and apprehension.

**God can work with apprehension, but He can't do much with "unbelief!"** Deborah and Havilah could have bowed in fear to unbelief, but instead they knelt in faith and stood up in boldness.

When Jesus went to minister in His hometown, the Bible says, "And because of their unbelief, he couldn't do any mighty miracles among them except to place his hands on a few sick people and heal them."[76] **Faith is a room lifter! Unbelief is a room killer! For Jesus, healing a few sick people is "no big deal." Apprehension doesn't amaze Him, but unbelief does. The next verse says, "He was amazed at their unbelief."[77]**

**Would to God we were all amazed at our unbelief! After all God has done for each of us, our unbelief shouldn't just amaze us, it should break our hearts, and make us cry out like the man whose son was demonized, "I believe; help my unbelief!"[78]**

---

**SCRIPTURE** *"I will give you a mouth and wisdom, which none of your adversaries will be able to withstand or contradict." (Luke 21:15)*

76. MARK 6:5, NKJV
77. MARK 6:6, NKJV
78. MARK 9:24, NKJV

# THE GREATEST MIRACLES I EVER SAW

**PRINCIPLE:** WE ARE THE PROJECT GOD CARES MOST ABOUT.

Have you ever felt like God set you up to fail? The greatest miracles I've ever seen took place in media projects that God never intended me to complete. Try filing that away!

It would take me years to fully process what had gone on and come to terms with God's ultimate intention for each life-altering situation. Even though today I am completely at peace with the death of those projects, in the past it was not always so. It seemed not only out of character for God to allow such mixed messages, but emotionally criminal. I was convinced my appeal to a higher court in Heaven would certainly receive a different verdict. But, for what seemed an eternity, my petitions were unanswered.

**God always defaults to what is ultimately in our best interest and therefore has no intention of fulfilling all of our dreams.** We are the project God cares most about! As the One who shaped and fashioned our inner needs, why would God fulfill a dream He knew was inherently unfulfilling? It took me half a lifetime to realize that His commitment is to fulfill His dream for me, which is infinitely better, though inevitably hidden from my eyes.

"It is God's privilege to conceal things and the king's privilege to discover them."[79] God's motive in this high-stakes game of hide-and-seek is pure and purposeful, though our experience on earth can be, at times, extremely painful. Many, who have gone through unexplainable tragedy, often arriving at a life-altering crossroad with a broken heart, have come to a far different conclusion about the motive of God.

**But God is not some cosmic killjoy getting His jollies out of pulling the wings off of helpless humans. In fact, quite the opposite is true. Once you see His heart and wisdom, you realize it is impossible for a blameless God to do anything but good.**

**SCRIPTURE** *"And in every matter of wisdom and understanding about which the king inquired of them, he found them ten times better than all the magicians and enchanters that were in all his kingdom. (Daniel 1:20)*

79. PROVERBS 25:2, NLT

**PRINCIPLE:** NO MATTER HOW BLEAK THE SITUATION, YOU ARE NOT BEYOND GOD'S PURPOSE AND PLAN FOR YOUR LIFE.

**There was a time in my Christian life when I struggled getting out of bed. It's embarrassing to say it, but true nonetheless.** My perspectives about God and my life were in need of a complete overhaul. I thought I needed my circumstances to change before I could feel good about my life. The truth was, I needed to trust that God had my life in His hands and that He would make all things work for my good if I loved Him and was committed to His will more than my will.

**Once I began to trust that God, as a loving Father, would never allow my life to be unfruitful, it changed my entire perspective.** Now, I bound out of bed every morning in the dark to walk in the light! I love my life because I believe God loves my life.

All of us will, at times, feel fractured and fragmented. So broken we wonder if our hearts and lives can ever be repaired and made whole. But once we understand God's heart, we realize that He will never discard us, but instead will gather us to Himself.

After Jesus multiplied the loaves and fishes, He said to pick up all of the fragments, the broken pieces, because they were important and not to be discarded. The Bible says, "And when they had eaten their fill, he told his disciples, 'Gather up the leftover fragments, that nothing may be lost.'" That nothing may be lost! WOW! That comforts me, as I often feel lost. But He is my Hero...my Rescuer!

**Learn to rest so completely in God's perfection that you're not overwhelmed by your own lack. Waiting for a better life is like staring at your dinner, hoping to improve its taste. The magnificent life God created for you...it's what's for dinner.**

**SCRIPTURE** *"We were crushed and completely overwhelmed...never live through it."* *(2Corinthians 1:8)*

80. ROMANS 8:28
81. JOHN 6:12, ESV

# JESUS PLUS NOTHING IS EVERYTHING

**PRINCIPLE:** WE CAN LOSE EVERYTHING,
BUT WE WILL NEVER LOSE JESUS.

I have this one goal in life. It's a grand goal and may surprise you, because it sounds a little funny to say, but I believe it anyway. "I want to be so at rest, so completely at peace in my heart, that when people see me, they feel like they're looking into the face of Jesus."

There, I've said it! It's a lofty hope, I know. But, I really believe it's not just achievable, but that it's God's will for my life. To represent Him so well, that everyone would want what I have: a deeply personal and magnificent relationship with Jesus Christ, my Lord and Savior. As Paul the Apostle wrote, "...that I may know him and the power of his resurrection, and may share his sufferings, becoming like him in his death, that by any means possible I may attain the resurrection from the dead."[82]

**Our thoughts about God will affect how we view life.**

**Do we see the magnificence of God? How extraordinary He is?**

**Or do we lose sight of Him and minimize His influence?**

Wouldn't the God who made sunsets and starry nights know something about beauty? Wouldn't the One who created laughter know how to have fun? Wouldn't the Prince of Peace help us rest? And, wouldn't the One who made puppies and babies know all about cute? God created sensual pleasure: the eye to behold beauty, the ear to enjoy music, the nose to embrace the fragrance of flowers, and a wonderful taste for food. But best of all, wouldn't the God who is love know all about relationships? That's because a relationship with Him is what we are looking for. He is everything we are longing for!

**Jesus plus nothing is everything, because only He knows what we truly need and only He can fully meet that need.**

---

**SCRIPTURE** *"For in Him (Jesus) dwells all the fullness of the Godhead bodily; and you are complete in Him..." (Colossians 2:9-10, NKJV)*

82. PHILIPPIANS 3:10-11

GRAB THE WHEEL OR DIE  | 1995 |

**PRINCIPLE:** OUR DECISION TO DO THE RIGHT THING MAY BE EMBARRASSING, YET NECESSARY.

Because I live on the West Coast of the U.S., whenever I fly to the East Coast to minister, I always lose three hours of sleep. On one occasion, I was picked up by the elderly father of a pastor to speak in multiple services. He was a stately man and very nice, but as we drove, I gradually became concerned about our safety.

While driving on a two-lane, elevated levy, he passed a car but remained in the oncoming traffic lane. When a car appeared on the horizon, I assumed he would certainly turn in. But, as the seconds passed, he did not. Finally, in desperation, I grabbed the wheel, pulling us back into our lane. It was incredibly embarrassing, and I immediately began to apologize.

A couple of minutes later, still mortified by what had just transpired and wondering if I had overreacted, the senior saint was about to enter a freeway with a sign reading "WRONG DIRECTION". This time I yelled, "Sir, please pull over!" I then drove us to the church and had the terrible task of explaining to the pastor, whom I had just met, what had transpired.

**It drove home this essential reality: sometimes we need to be bold enough to leave where we are in order to get to where we need to be.** The Bible says, "By faith Abraham obeyed when he was called to go out to the place which he would receive as an inheritance. And he went out, not knowing where he was going. By faith he dwelt in the land of promise..."[83]

**Abraham went after his inheritance. We have to go after our future. It's not going to come to us. We'll have to leave the security of the known for the unknown. Sure, it will take obedience, faith, and courage, but in the end we'll see that what God had in mind is better than what we can imagine. Take a leap of faith into God's will. It's the safest place to be.**

---

**SCRIPTURE** *"The fear of man lays a snare, but whoever trusts in the Lord is safe."* (Proverbs 29:25)

83. HEBREWS 11:8–9A, NKJV

**PRINCIPLE:** THERE ARE SERIOUS CONSEQUENCES FOR RESISTING GOD'S WILL.

Fifteen years after Morning Star Ranch closed, a former resident tracked me down at a low point in his life. During our intense conversation, he confessed he had become a "hit man" and now wanted to get right with God. After hours with him, our discussion settled on the reality that, if he were genuinely repentant, he would need to take full responsibility for his actions, and this would have legal ramifications.

At that time, the Sheriff in our town attended our church, and I offered to set up a meeting so he could turn himself in. Though, at one point, he acknowledged his need to "bear fruit in keeping with repentance," ultimately he reneged on doing the right thing. Repentance always requires the dual miracle of God's forgiveness and man changing his mind.

After a spirited back and forth, he threatened, as he put it, "Maybe, I'll just do you!"

I refused to be intimidated! Whether I live or die, I am the Lord's and no one can take that away from me. His final words, right before he walked out and the door closed behind him were, "You're everything I wanted to be!" It was tragic!

**I've never been everything I wanted to be, but cling to "The steadfast love of the Lord (that) never ceases; his mercies (that) never come to an end; (for) they are new every morning; great is your faithfulness.."**

Does humility diminish us, or elevate us? Paul the Apostle acknowledged the truth. "I was once a blasphemer and a persecutor and a violent man..." He even went so far as to say he was the "chief of sinners." But then he mentions God's response to this confession; but "I was shown mercy because I acted in ignorance and unbelief."[88]

**If I think I'm really not that bad, I'm in denial, and I've never really seen my life from God's perspective. We all need a Savior, and thankfully, Jesus is ready and willing to save a repentant heart.**

---

**SCRIPTURE** *"...unholy like Esau, who sold his birthright for a single meal. For you know that afterward, when he desired to inherit the blessing, he was rejected, for he found no chance to repent, though he sought it with tears." (Hebrews 12:16b-17)*

84. MATTHEW 3:8
85. LAMENTATIONS 3:22-23
86. 1TIMOTHY 1:13A, NIV
87. 1TIMOTHY 1:15
88. 1TIMOTHY 1:13B, NIV

# DEBORAH THE DREAMER

**PRINCIPLE:** GOD HAS GIVEN EACH OF US A COMBINATION OF GIFTS NO ONE ELSE HAS.

When my daughter Deborah was about six years old, we went for a walk in the Oregon woods. It wasn't until it was getting dark that I realized I was lost. Sadly, it doesn't take much for that to happen. So I said, "Deborah, I think we're lost!" She said, "I know how to get us back." I knelt down and looked at her for a very long time. She was six years old, three-feet nothing! She could barely tie her shoes. So I said, "Are you absolutely sure, Deborah?" She said, "Yep!"

And so, as it was getting really dark, she took me by the hand and led me out of those "dark, scary woods." It was the beginning of a significant revelation: **the next generation will be leading us before we know it, and it will be a good thing.**

God gives gifts to each of us that are perfectly tailored to our persona: our personality, temperament, gifting, etc. **Since Deborah was a teenager, God has given her dreams: big, detailed, colorful and specific! Not predominantly for her, but for others. They have provided milestones of direction with divine insight for key leaders.** Deborah's personality is unassuming, happy to be in the background, but capable of being strong and making a decision. She is willing to humbly undergird the gifts in others, which only adds to her credibility. She's not prone to self-promotion, rather, she has a genuine excitement when others are honored or valued. I respect Deborah a lot!

But this dream thing she's been given thunders into prominence; especially when it solves a riddle, or provides long-term direction for leaders as it has on many occasions.

There have been times when Deborah is with friends and she happens to mention casually, "I had this dream last night..." not thinking it had any relevance to those around her, because it may have just been the pizza. But, she realizes pretty quickly that the entire table has gotten stone quiet, until she says, "No, it's not that kind of dream," followed by nervous laughter. **The gifts and callings of God are always a really BIG deal!**

---

**SCRIPTURE** *"Philip the evangelist, who was one of the seven, and stayed with him. He had four unmarried daughters, who prophesied." (Acts 21:8–9) "Now Deborah, a prophetess...was judging Israel at that time." (Judges 4:4)*

# HAVILAH
## THE PREACHER

**PRINCIPLE:**  WHEN MAN SAYS, "LIMITED!" GOD SAYS, "LIMITLESS!"

My daughter Havilah grew up with learning disabilities: school was a chore and studying was a nuisance. She was very bright, just not academic. But, no one was more persistent than Havilah. She would always say, "I can do it!" even before she found out what "it" was. Consequently, I would say, "Havilah is a lion, and the lion won't turn aside for anything!"[89]

We told both Havilah and Deborah that they were leaders, even before they could walk, praying empowering prayers over them every night as we laid our hands on their foreheads. "Lord, we thank you that you have made Deborah and Havilah leaders!"

So, it was no surprise that Havilah learned to first lead worship and then to preach. But what was stunning was her ability to write books, produce videos and devotionals, and speak with such authority and anointing. She cultivated the gifts God had given her, and now thousands around the world are receiving the benefit of her diligence.

One day, when Havilah was a teenager, she told me God had spoken to her about me. She said, "You know Dad, how you feel like right now you're not seeing all of the success you'd like to see right now? Well, right now Deborah and I are your success." The car rides got really misty at that point, and after a few seconds composing myself, I responded, "I really do know that, sweetheart, but sometimes I just lose sight of it, and need to hear it again."

Did you ever notice that God encourages us with Bible heroes who are just as weak as we are? Moses felt disqualified because of his past failures. He said, "Who am I?"[90] Gideon retorted, "How can I save Israel? My clan's the weakest, and I'm the least in my family."[91] When God told Sarah she would have a baby in her old age, she laughed in unbelief.[92] The prophet Jeremiah complained, "I can't speak for you! I'm too young!"[93] God responded: "Don't be afraid! I will deliver you! I have put My words in your mouth."[94]

**Even Jesus struggled with the fact that, like David and Joseph, His brothers didn't believe in His calling.[95] Yet, called He was, and so are you. Never forget, once given, God's gifts and callings cannot be taken from you...by anyone.[96] Our inabilities don't have to keep us from fulfilling God's will.**

---

**SCRIPTURE** *"A river flowed from the land of Eden, watering the garden and then dividing into four branches. The first branch, called the Pishon, flowed around the entire land of Havilah, where gold is found. The gold of that land is exceptionally pure; aromatic resin and onyx stone are also found there." (Genesis 2:10–12)*

89. PROVERBS 30:30, NLT   90. EXODUS 3:11
91. JUDGES 6:15, NIV   92. GENESIS 18:12
93. JEREMIAH 1:6, NLT   94. JEREMIAH 1:8–9
95. JOHN 7:5   96. ROMANS 11:29

# SUPERNATURAL GENEROSITY

**PRINCIPLE:** EVERYTHING WE HAVE BEEN GIVEN IS ACTUALLY A GIFT FROM GOD AND OTHERS.

**When I saw selfless giving modeled for me, I knew it was the high ground.** Even when I tended to have spiritual amnesia, God would allow me to see someone like Himself: a Giver. The church that sent us out to plant The Rock of Roseville, Glad Tidings, in Yuba City, CA, lavishly gave people and resources to start our church. The Rock of Gainesville in Florida, demonstrated generous giving so profoundly, it made me cry, and caused us to name our church after them.

When our opportunity at The Rock of Roseville came to plant churches, my mantra was, "Everyone can go except Suzie." I know, that was pretty selfish of me. We sowed 500 people, in three church plants, giving away as much as 40% of our income to one of them. To another, we sowed 250 people, and let them grow, one block away from us. Part of the impetus for all of this were good and bad examples. Some leaders and churches inspired me; others saddened me. But I learned from both!

**We can either be rushing rivers of blessing, washing over all who come in contact with us, or stagnant ponds of entitlement, misrepresenting the giving heart of God.**

In the gospels, a grateful woman broke a jar of very costly perfume and anointed Jesus.[97] Judging from the response of His disciples, you would have thought she broke the jar over His head. Some of those present said indignantly, "Why this waste of perfume? It could have been sold for more than a year's wages and the money given to the poor."[98] How much do you make in a year? Can you imagine giving it away in one day? Her action was an incredibly sacrificial gesture. That's why Jesus said, "Leave her alone. Why are you bothering her? She has done a beautiful thing to me...She did what she could."[99]

**Her gracious action makes me ask the following question: What is Jesus asking us to do for Him, that He would consider beautiful?**

---

**SCRIPTURE** *"Whoever brings blessing will be enriched, and one who waters will himself be watered." (Proverbs 11:25)*

97. MARK 14:3
98. MARK 14:4-5
99. MARK 14:6,8

# SUIT RUINED BECAUSE OF MAKEUP AND TEARS

1998

**PRINCIPLE:** THE NEXT GENERATION IS LOOKING FOR SAFE PARENTS MORE THAN WE CAN IMAGINE.

A few years ago, my dear friend Pastor George Brantley was invited to speak to a thousand students at Christ For the Nations in Dallas, Texas. He is one of the greatest fathers I have ever known. After spending two days lovingly sharing about the "Fathering" principle, he invited anyone who needed a "safe hug" to come forward.

What happened next was both tragic and astounding. Hundreds of young men and women lined up for three hours to receive a "safe hug." Some said, "I have never received a hug from either my father or mother." One after another, they sobbed on George's shoulders, literally ruining his jacket and shirt. That's the kind of desperate hunger for safe, godly fathers people have.

I once met a man who shared that he hadn't seen his only son in twelve years. When I tried to comfort him, he shot back brashly, "It's his loss, not mine!" It was so sad! **He had invented an imaginary reality to soothe an unbearable sadness. I found it revealing that he knew exactly how long it had been since he had spoken to his son.**

**God can repair every breach, heal our family divisions, and reconcile broken relationships. The Bible calls Jesus the "repairer of the breach."**[100] That's even why the Father sent Jesus: to heal broken hearts,[101] and why He has now called each of us to be His "ministers of reconciliation."[102] In a world filled with pain, God wants to use us to help heal others. The Bible says, "...because Jesus lives forever...he is able...to save those who come to God through him. He lives forever to intercede with God on their behalf."[103]

**I don't ever want to stop loving people, because I know God will never stop loving me.**

---

**SCRIPTURE** *"Rejoice with those who rejoice, weep with those who weep." (Romans 12:15)*

100. ISAIAH 58:12
101. LUKE 4:18
102. 2CORINTHIANS 5:18
103. HEBREWS 7:24-25, NLT

# POLICE AND FIRE BANQUET IN OUR CITY

**PRINCIPLE:** HONOR IS A QUALITY THAT IS HARD TO FIND, YET SO DESPERATELY NEEDED.

In 1999, we were inspired to champion a City Awards Banquet for the Police and Fire Departments in our city of Roseville, California.[104] It was two years before the terrorist attack of September 11, 2001 and, when this occurred, the necessity of honoring our public servants was only magnified. Year after year, churches and businesses helped sponsor this event that allowed our police officers and fire fighters, with their families, to know they were valued and appreciated.

In 2016, we added a larger City Awards Celebration[105] honoring the Police Department in Sacramento, of which Roseville is a suburb. Taking the lead from this initiative were multi-racial churches, realizing that we must build bridges of mutual respect, so that in the event divisive situations arise in our community, relationships will already be in place to navigate the difficulties we will face.

My initial discussion about having a City Award Celebration for our police department began during a 45-minute walk with Sacramento's Police Chief Sam Somers during the 2014 MLK March for the Dream.[106] This is one of America's largest MLK marches, with 25,000 people, and follows our annual MLK Celebration.[107] It would, however, take two and a half years to rally churches in the Sacramento region. We were particularly honored that African-American pastors took the lead in making this Celebration a reality. **When the leadership pieces finally were in place to have the honor evening, the relationship between police and some African-American communities across America was so toxic we knew an event like this was critical.**

With only three months to plan and raise the $50,000 needed, we set a date and prayed for rain. Less than three weeks before the gathering, we had only $4,000 pledged. Then, after sharing an impassioned appeal to pray for Sacramento to fulfill her destiny as a breakout city for the healing of our nation, someone committed to fund the entire event...$50,000. The God of the supernatural had once again been faithful to "supply all of our need."[108]

Historically, in cities across America, church steeples lined town squares, and the parson, meaning the *person*, was seen as a pillar in his community. With the secularization of our society, the church and its leaders have been marginalized and their role in unifying communities diminished. But, if, as Jesus said, we are called to be salt and light in our communities,[109] then we must learn to be servant leaders like Jesus, for we were created to be conformed to His image and likeness.[110]

**SCRIPTURE** *"Let every person be subject to the governing authorities. For there is no authority except from God, and those that exist have been instituted by God. Therefore, whoever resists the authorities resists what God has appointed, and those who resist will incur judgment." (Romans 13:1–3)*

104. ROSEVILLECITYAWARDS.COM
105. CITYAWARDSHUB.COM
106. MLK365.ORG
107. MLKSACRAMENTO.COM
108. PHILIPPIANS 4:19
109. MATTHEW 5:13–16
110. ROMANS 8:29

# THERE'S NO BAD NEWS IN GOD

**PRINCIPLE:** THERE IS NO BAD NEWS, IF WE LOVE GOD AND ARE COMMITTED TO DO HIS WILL.

A key church staff member came into my office years ago with a sad look on his face and said, "I have some bad news. We have a very serious problem!" A few minutes later, when I was alone and was able to prayerfully consider our situation, the Holy Spirit spoke to my heart and gave me a crystal clear commission. "Francis, you are in charge of the 'Respond Well Department;' I am in charge of everything else."

WOW! It was a lightning bolt revelation! God was guiding me to a place of both wisdom and peace. He was affirming the reality that: Either He is in charge or He is not! Either God is able, or He is not! He alone promises, "...to do exceedingly abundantly above all that we ask or think, according to the power that works in us..."[111]

Who is the author of your decisions? God? Or you?

Frankly, I've learned to try and not make decisions.

For years, whenever I had a strong preference, I'd get in trouble. So, I solved it. I don't make the decisions! Now, I want my only preference to be God's will. Frankly, I'd have to know the future and all possibilities to make a decision based upon what I know. With God as the sole decision-maker, I experience far less pressure.

**In the past, as soon as I began to personalize my situation and my circumstances, I took charge and ran ahead of God, rather than flow with His Spirit. It didn't make any difference if my preference was a "good thing" or a "bad thing," unless God authored it, He wasn't going to finish it. As a result of these insights, I've learned to spend my time focusing on obeying God, leaving my personal preferences aside.**

**Trust God! He will guide your every step, if you'll let Him.**

---

**SCRIPTURE** *"Those who are righteous will be long remembered. They do not fear bad news; they confidently trust the Lord to care for them." (Psalm 112:6-7)*

111. EPHESIANS 3:20, NKJV

# THE
# PASTORAL
*2000–2008* # YEARS

# THE PASTORAL
*2000–2008* YEARS

OUR WONDERFUL FAMILY

PASTORS DON AND CHRISTA PROCTOR

MY BEAUTIFUL WIFE SUZIE

SO GRATEFUL ALL MY SIBLINGS KNOW JESUS    PRAYING AT THE WAILING WALL

OUR DEAR FRIENDS, AND FELLOW PASTORS, BOB AND LADONNA HASTY

CELEBRATING MY 60TH BIRTHDAY

GRANDKIDS: WILLIAM, GABRIELLA, HUDSON AND JUDAH

MY BEAUTIFUL GIRLS!

# "I DON'T WANT TO APPEAR TO BE CONTROLLING"

**PRINCIPLE:** UNHEALED WOUNDS CAN CAUSE UNKNOWN AND DISTORTED PERSPECTIVES.

In 2000, a dear friend of mine, Pastor George Brantley, was a guest speaker at our church. He is one of the best fathers I know, both with his own three sons and with the men and women of his great congregation, The Rock of Gainesville, in Gainesville, Florida. It was during George's stay with us that the Holy Spirit revealed an unhealthy perspective in my heart.

Just before George spoke, I was describing to our congregation that my primary role as their pastor was as a coach. I thought nothing of my comments until later that day when, during lunch, George gently commented he was surprised I had presented my role to the church as primarily being a coach and not a father. I quickly responded, "I refer to myself as a coach, and not a father, because I don't want them to feel I am being controlling."

Even as the words left my mouth, I knew they were deformed. Why would I assume the mere mention of my being a father would connote an overbearing attitude toward those I am called to serve? As I thought and prayed about my comments, I realized I was presenting myself as a coach because I didn't want to even appear to be overly controlling, as my father had been. My wounded past had distorted my present perspective.

It grieved me tremendously and made me shudder wondering what other misguided perceptions I harbored in my soul. I had never felt fully capable of being a spiritual father, even though I knew I was called to be one. A little while after this monumental, personal epiphany, I polled our church during weekend services: What role would you like me to have as your pastor: Coach, CEO, Older Brother, or Father? **An overwhelming 70% in each of the weekend services voted for Father. It broke me again!**

**I then publicly asked our church's forgiveness for in some way misrepresenting God's heart. This revelation and my subsequent repentance brought a further level of healing to the father wounds in my own life and, I believe, in the lives of many others in our congregation.**

**SCRIPTURE** *"For though you have countless guides in Christ, you do not have many fathers. For I became your father in Christ Jesus through the gospel." (1Corinthians 4:15)*

# GETTING PAST GUARDS IN COMMUNIST CHINA

**PRINCIPLE:** IT WILL TAKE GREAT COURAGE TO FACE YOUR FEARS AND THE INTIMIDATION OF OTHERS.

In 2000, thirty members of our church family went on a mission trip to Tibet, a nation high in the Himalayas. Due to the fact that Lhasa, its capital, was located at 14,500 feet, one of the greatest dangers was altitude sickness. Even our tour guide, who grew up in Tibet, had her father die of this illness.

As we were about to leave, my daughter, Havilah, and Shannon, a daughter of a close friend, got really sick with altitude sickness. They were so ill, we literally carried them onto the plane and administered oxygen. Our flight out of Tibet took us to Chengdu, a city in southern China, and from there we were to fly to Hong Kong. But, their condition deteriorated so severely, we sought medical attention after our first flight. The medical personnel at the airport were alarmed, and called for an ambulance.

As Havilah and Shannon lay on the ground in serious condition, God supernaturally led an American nurse, who had just come from Base Camp at Mount Everest, and who was knowledgeable about altitude sickness, to examine them. She was very concerned! Looking directly into my eyes, she said sternly, "You need to get these ladies on that flight! Do not let them go to the hospital here! They will get much better care in Hong Kong!"

With that commission, we took them by wheelchair to our flight, but were stopped by soldiers and airport officials who insisted they go to a hospital. The look in the American nurse's eyes made this option unthinkable! Not knowing how things would turn out, we barreled our way forward, insisting that we were all going on the flight. It was wild! Our will against theirs, we muscled our way onto the plane. I'm absolutely persuaded that God sent that American nurse, giving us the clarity we needed to make this hard decision.

**Irritations are divine opportunities, not stumbling blocks or roadblocks. If we obsess over the pain and displeasure inherently associated with the struggles of life, we'll miss their entire point. The real enemy is never the things happening around us, it's our poor response. By the grace of God, we each have a complete capacity to respond well and the courage to face any fears that come.**

**There are no setbacks in God, only veiled doorways to our destiny.**

**SCRIPTURE** *"The angel of the Lord encamps around those who fear Him and delivers them." (Psalm 34:7)*

# FIRST HOLE-IN-ONE BRINGS HORRIBLE CONNECTION

**PRINCIPLE:** GOD'S WISDOM IS A DEMONSTRATION OF HIS MARVELOUS GRACE.

On September 3, 2001, I was playing golf. On the 8th hole, I got my first hole-in-one. Immediately, I knew it had spiritual significance. God spoke to my heart that it was a new beginning. So, the next weekend, I spoke about a "New Beginning." It certainly would be, but not in the way I was thinking. Two days after my message, the World Trade Center was destroyed by terrorists. We all know how traumatic that was, and still is. It was the beginning of a whole new phase for our nation and even our world.

God had used a natural phenomenon to speak to me. Throughout my Christian life, He has at times ordered my steps in many supernatural ways, but I've endeavored to only see their significance in retrospect, not in advance. I wouldn't go to the store for milk based on a prophetic word, but I have received profound insights from hundreds of prophetic encouragements over the years.

What is the secret to finding out the will of God? First, start by realizing you don't know it. Then as James writes, "If any of you lack wisdom…" (That would be all of us!) "…let him ask God."[112] The Bible says, "Wisdom is the principal thing. Therefore get wisdom."[113] **Our asking God for wisdom should be like breathing—a moment-by-moment expression of our need for Him. We think we know what's best, but we don't!**

**God's Plan "A" is often our Plan "B" or "C" or even "Z."**

**If we trust God, even worst case scenarios have a silver lining! And that silver lining is called grace, accessed by faith, and planted in each of our hearts. "Jesus, give me the faith to always believe that you not only know best, but that You are activating Your best for my life, even now."**

---

**SCRIPTURE** *"Behold, the former things have come to pass, and new things I now declare; before they spring forth I tell you of them." (Isaiah 42:9)*

112. JAMES 1:5
113. PROVERBS 4:7

# HEALING CAR RIDE IN HEAVEN

**PRINCIPLE:** GOD THE FATHER'S DESIRE IS ALWAYS FOR HEALING AND RESTORATION.

When I was a young Christian, one of my former pastors and spiritual fathers was very abusive. I was a leader in his church. He wounded me deeply, openly ridiculing me before the entire church, my friends and my family. So many times, I drove around town listening to worship music while crying uncontrollably. I felt like I was near a nervous breakdown. I couldn't stop crying. Before the ridicule began, God challenged me to respond well, so I remained silent in spite of the accusations.

Many years later, as the senior pastor of a church myself, I had a dream about him. In the dream, we were driving along in heaven. It was majestically beautiful with brilliant colors and complete peace. I turned to him in the passenger seat still full of hurt over the things he had said and done. Without any anger or vindictiveness in my heart, I looked into his eyes and asked, "Why did you do it?"

His face was sad but steady. Looking down in embarrassment, and then back up into my eyes, a gentle, understanding smile came on his face. Reaching out and hugging me, he said, "It doesn't make a difference anymore." And I knew it was true.

As we hugged, there was an explosion of love in my heart like nothing I have ever experienced on earth. The dream ended. I woke up sobbing in my bed in the middle of the night. **Some deep, supernatural inner healing had taken place. Though I had forgiven and released him hundreds of times, over many years, I was suddenly freer than I had ever been toward him. It was a glimpse of heaven and God's forgiving love I will never forget.**

**Will you completely forgive those who have hurt you? Will you release them? You may have to pray hundreds of times, but the healing will be well worth it.**

**SCRIPTURE** *"The Spirit of the Lord is upon me...to proclaim that captives will be released, that the blind will see, that the oppressed will be set free, and that the time of the Lord's favor has come." (Luke 4:18–19, NLT)*

**PRINCIPLE:**  GOD COULD NOT POSSIBLY LOVE AND LIKE US
MORE THAN HE ALREADY DOES.

Do you like the sound of your voice? God does! The Bible says, "The LORD hears His people when they call to Him for help."[114] Growing up, I didn't like the way my voice sounded. I wanted it to be deeper, richer. Now, I find it ironic that I'm on radio. God's got a great sense of humor. But it also demonstrates that God is far more gracious than critical. He focuses on what really matters. The Bible says, "The LORD doesn't see things the way you see them. People judge by outward appearance, but the LORD looks at the heart."[115] Maybe, if God likes the sound of my voice, I should like it also. Let me take it one step further. If God likes me, I should like me too.

In early 2003, as I spent many hours soaking in God's presence at the International House of Prayer in Kansas City, God did a tremendous work in my heart that continues today. I experienced a closeness to Jesus I had not felt since I first received Him in 1972. There were also powerful teachings about God's fascination for us: how we captivate His heart. Over time, they opened my eyes to see that God doesn't just love us; He genuinely likes and enjoys us; not everything we do, but everything we are to Him. In the deepest part of my being I sensed God's complete acceptance with no disappointment or sense of failure—only the joy of a lost son being fully restored to his Father. All I could do was receive God's loving embrace.

**When you consider what God thinks of you, does it make you sad or glad? Your answer will define your whole life. Do you make God smile or frown?**

It's not just possible to know the answer to these questions; it's essential that we do. I'm convinced God makes a distinction between who I am to Him, and my sin. The sinful actions that distort my true identity do not and cannot separate me from His love.

Frankly, there's nothing I could ever do to make God love me more or less than He already does. Therefore, my feeling better about myself should never be based upon my performance. Yes, we still sin! But, because Jesus died for our sins, our God-intended identity is not that of a sinner, but as a son.

---

**SCRIPTURE** *"In this is love, not that we have loved God but that he loved us and sent his Son to be the propitiation for our sins." (1John 4:10)*

114. PSALM 34:17, NLT
115. 1SAMUEL 16:7, NLT

# NO SUCCESS WITHOUT A HOUSE OF PRAYER

**PRINCIPLE:** ALL WE ARE HOPING FOR CAN ONLY COME THROUGH A RELATIONSHIP WITH GOD.

In 2002, God emphatically shared with me that I would not see success in what I was believing for, without a House of Prayer. A conversation with my dear friend, Mike Grant, reconnected me with Diane Hallam, a dear friend who had worked with me for many years as my Executive Assistant at Christian Equippers International, in South Lake Tahoe. She had been at IHOP-KC, teaching on the Song of Solomon, and so we invited her to come help us launch a House of Prayer. It is where she met her husband, Nick Parnell. Together, they have been Directors of our House of Prayer for many years.

**I could not do what I do without intercessors and the House of Prayer. I would even go so far as to say that we would not be seeing many of the breakthroughs we have seen in the Sacramento region without RHOP, the Rock House of Prayer.**

Do you have a burden to pray? If you do, it didn't start as your burden. It started with God. We don't pray to get God's attention; we pray because God has gotten ours. I've never initiated anything of eternal value. If I happened to strike everlasting gold, it's because God shook me hard enough to awaken me to do His will. The Bible says, "Awake, O sleeper, rise up from the dead, and Christ will give you light."[116] I want to live fully awake. I want to die fully awake. I want to pray what's on God's heart, for only then will my prayers be answered.

We were each made to have an exciting, adventurous love relationship with our Creator. He wants to romance us! To sweep us off our feet! To take us to heavenly places, places He created with us in mind. Pursue the Lover we were created for, Who says, "I have loved you with an everlasting love."[117] "This is love: not that we loved God, but that He loved us and sent his Son as an atoning sacrifice for our sins."[118]

---

**SCRIPTURE** *"...I will bring to my holy mountain, and make them joyful in my house of prayer; their burnt offerings and their sacrifices will be accepted on my altar, for my house shall be called a house of prayer for all peoples." (Isaiah 56:7)*

116. EPHESIANS 5:14, NLT
117. JEREMIAH 31:3, NIV
118. 1JOHN 4:10, NIV

THE "FRANCIS GENERATOR" PROPHECY

**PRINCIPLE:** WE CAN NEVER FULFILL PROPHECIES, BUT WE MUST BE WILLING TO STEP INTO THEM.

In 2003, a commercial electrician sent me a video with a prophetic word. He filmed it inside the Folsom Dam, standing in front of a massive turbine called a "Francis Generator." It was named after James B. Francis, the inventor of the world's most commonly used turbine to generate hydroelectricity in large dam systems.

He prophesied that God was going to use me to affect the flow of life into the Sacramento Valley, which in turn would affect the valley's spiritual temperature and quality of life. I had no inkling about how this might happen, but I sensed the veracity of the word. Ironically, Folsom Dam was even dedicated on my spiritual birthday, May 14, 1956.

I've found there are two keys to prophetic words we should always remember: 1) There is nothing we can or should do to initiate them, but if we are obedient to the Spirit's promptings, we can see the hand of God bringing them to pass. 2) Just because we receive a prophetic word, doesn't mean we don't have to deal with fear.

**The fear of leading isn't new. Everyone fights its insidious grip, while few overcome it.** From feeble Lot who lost his family's respect, refusing to lead them out of a city that was being destroyed, to outspoken Peter warming himself by the fires of the world, denying Jesus, and weeping bitterly.

It will take courage to lead others toward what is eternally good in an age where most people willingly follow what they'll eventually realize was eternally bad. **At times we have to hate what we have become in order to embrace what we are meant to be. I want to live a safe life, but I don't want to live so safe I never rely completely on God.**

Mark Twain once wrote, "Twenty years from now you will be more disappointed by the things you didn't do than by the ones you did. So throw off the bowlines, sail away from the safe harbor, catch the trade winds in your sails. Explore. Dream. Discover." How true! We can stay close to the shore, and never launch out into the depth of God's great adventure. If we never break a nail, we likewise may never break free from the fear of the unknown, which may just be a lack of willingness to trust God. The Bible says, "Peter got out of the boat and walked on the water and came to Jesus."[119]

**We're always safer walking toward Jesus than cowering in the boat.**

**SCRIPTURE** *"But Mary treasured up all these things, pondering them in her heart."* (Luke 2:19)

119. MATTHEW 14:19

# HEART FOR THE FATHER-LESS AND MOTHERLESS

**PRINCIPLE:** ALLOWING GOD TO HEAL YOU BRINGS HEALING TO OTHERS.

All of us would rather show off our fruit than let others see where we've been pruned. But without the pruning we would eventually lose our dependency on the vine. Then, in time, we'd think we are the ones who produced the fruit, rather than the vine being our source. Jesus said, "Every branch in me that does not bear fruit he takes away, and every branch that does bear fruit he prunes, that it may bear more fruit."[120]

For many years I've had the privilege of ministering each month to forty young women in two wonderfully restorative communities, Mercy Ministries and Koinonia Group Foster Homes. All with emotional scars, many from their own parents. Once, they were asked to describe someone beautiful and tell what makes him or her so. They each agreed that true beauty is seen in someone willing to be authentic.

One young lady wrote, "What makes people beautiful is that they're always real. They're not afraid to be who they are—sharing their real emotions, feelings, thoughts, and ideas. They never play mind games and are always honest and candid. When I see a person living his or her life in this way, it makes me yearn to live my life that way also, and gives me the confidence to believe I can do so."

Jesus, make me that kind of person!

**Do you have father wounds or mother wounds? Though it is unsettling to retrieve the priceless value of past hurts, they are actually the birth pangs of renewed hope. Many of us have an unclaimed lottery ticket from our childhood in the pocket closest to our heart. Even though it will be painful, it is God's will that what was stolen from us is restored, not just in our own life, but also for generations to come.**

God can use the sadness in our past to help someone in our present. Every healed hurt in our lives offers hope to others. That's life's great irony: that every person takes what the devil meant for evil and sees it transformed into good. If we yield to God's Spirit, nothing is ever wasted in His Kingdom.

---

**SCRIPTURE** *"...he will turn the hearts of fathers to their children and the hearts of children to their fathers..." (Malachi 4:6)*

120. JOHN 15:2

# PAID A $25,000 DEBT WE DIDN'T OWE

**PRINCIPLE:** OBEDIENCE IS NOT ABOUT FAIRNESS. IT'S ALL ABOUT UNWAVERING DEVOTION TO GOD.

Many years ago, my wife Suzie and I were confronted with a perplexing decision. A businessman had taken $25,000 from his company's pension fund in order to invest in a project we were working on. When we found out, we were greatly troubled he had used money that wasn't his. Though it was a debt we didn't owe, we believed God wanted us to pay it back. Yet, being financially strapped ourselves, we were only able to give the company an average of $125 a month.

We did this faithfully for 11 years, prayerfully sowing the much-needed funds as an act of obedience. With 2 1/2 years and $8,500 left, I shared the story for the first time during a weekend message. The next morning, we received a letter saying the company had been dissolved, and that we didn't need to make any further payments. **The letter had been in the mail as I spoke and was such a sweet example of how God always honors obedience.**

It also demonstrates how to have a healthy walk with God. "For you were once darkness, but now you are light in the Lord. Walk as children of light."[121] Our walk with God is founded on either good or bad habits. And these habits can only be formed by disciplines. Our desires will come and go, but our habits will stick. Why? Because our habits will affect our future! It took trust, discipline and sacrifice for Suzie and I to pay a debt we didn't owe for 11 years. It was a good habit...but a hard habit!

What would you rather do: volunteer to do something, or do something because you're told to? It's no surprise that we'd all probably rather volunteer. Yet the Bible says, "to obey is better than sacrifice."[122] God's not looking for volunteers, He's looking for people who are willing to be obedient out of love for Him.

**God doesn't want us to be creative about His will. He wants us to do His will. He isn't looking for scriptwriters. He needs script-doers! We don't train our children to be volunteers. Our hope is that they'll learn to be obedient to us, and even more so to God. There are people waiting for us on the other side of our obedience, and only through obedience to Christ can we find our destiny and true identity.**

**SCRIPTURE** *"So where can you find someone truly wise, truly educated, truly intelligent in this day and age? Hasn't God exposed it all as pretentious nonsense? Since the world in all its fancy wisdom never had a clue when it came to knowing God." (1Corinthians 1:20, The Message)*

121. EPHESIANS 5:8, NKJV
122. 1SAMUEL 15:22, NKJV

**PRINCIPLE:** NO ONE WANTS TO ANSWER OUR GOD-INITIATED PRAYERS MORE THAN GOD.

The first time Suzie and I went to Israel, we spent time praying at the Wailing Wall in Jerusalem. It is believed to be the remains of a wall from the Second Jewish Temple expanded by King Herod in 19 B.C. It extends for about 62 feet (18.9 m) above the ground, and is considered a sacred site by Jews. Thousands of people make pilgrimages there each year and place tiny prayer petitions in its cracks. We did as well.

At that time, our twin daughters, Deborah and Havilah, had been married for a year or so, but had not yet gotten pregnant. Suzie placed a prayer request in the wall for grandchildren. When we returned home, thinking our house was unoccupied, we were greeted by a large sign with blue and pink balloons in our living room saying, "Welcome home Grandma and Grandpa!" Our daughters and their husbands, Daniel and Ben, then came out of the bedroom rejoicing! We thought only one of them was newly pregnant, but instead they both were, and gave birth nine days apart to Judah and Gabriella.

In the Old Testament the children of Israel carried a chest with them called the Ark of the Covenant, or the Ark of the Testimony. **It contained three items that reminded them, and even us today, who God is and all He has done.**

1) The Ten Commandment tablets given to Moses upon which God wrote laws showing how to live safe and healthy lives. 2) Aaron's rod (that budded) that God used to perform miracles when He delivered the Israelites from Pharaoh in ancient Egypt. 3) A jar of manna, the food God rained down from heaven when the children of Israel were in the wilderness for 40 years. **All three of these objects assure us that God will provide for our every need, even when we struggle to find our way**.

**It may surprise you that our prayers never initiate God moving in our lives or in those around us. NEVER! It is His heart that awakens us to pray for what He knows is best for us. We are never the initiator! God is always the author and finisher of everything that is eternal and good. What God begins, He finishes!**

**SCRIPTURE** *Jesus said, "Until now you have asked nothing in my name. Ask, and you will receive, that your joy may be full." (John 16:24)*

# LIVING WITH THE FAVOR OF GOD

**PRINCIPLE:** PAST SEEDS OF OBEDIENCE ALWAYS REAP AN EXCEPTIONAL FUTURE HARVEST.

I was using the word "success" in relation to God with one of my daughters, Havilah, when she said, "You know Dad, even though I know what you mean, a better word to use is the word "favor." I loved her recommendation, and when I looked up its definition, it only got better. **Favor is defined as "support or advancement given as a sign of approval, overgenerous preferential treatment, and an act of kindness beyond what is due." WOW! Isn't that what God does for us? How would our experience of life change if we viewed every challenge as a promotion, every struggle as an opportunity, and every difficulty as divinely ordained by God. If we really trusted that a loving, gracious, generous God had planned the best life possible for each of us, we'd live in peace beyond our understanding; fully embracing His favor.**

Before I began to pastor in 1997, my wife Suzie and I traveled for 18 years, speaking in hundreds of churches. What we saw changed our lives and shaped our future. The best qualities, seen in the healthiest people and churches, were the premiere representations of Jesus Christ we'd ever seen. They became our church values, but I believe they are also great values for each of us to live by.

Here they are: Be grateful for who God is, and what He's done. He will fill your life with joy. Allow God's Spirit and Word to make you whole, so you can fulfill His destiny. Following Jesus is more about action than words. Be committed to love, give, serve, and honor those God brings your way. And lastly, be accountable to others, so you can finish well.

My wife and I are not shrewd business people. Our only hope in making wise financial decisions is in sowing obedient seed, and then discerning God's will. In 2004, before the recession hit, God encouraged us to sell our home. We did, and were able to reap a 135% profit. It paid for our daughter's weddings and provided a nest egg for our future.

**"For you bless the righteous, O LORD; you cover him with favor as with a shield."[123]**

---

**SCRIPTURE** *"The blessing of the Lord makes rich, and he adds no sorrow with it."* *(Proverbs 10:22)*

123. PSALM 5:12

# MALARIA, DEBILITATION, AND MY UNLIKELY HEALING

**PRINCIPLE:** GOD CAN USE AN UNLIKELY MEANS TO BRING ABOUT THE HEALING WE NEED.

By the grace of God, I've always been healthy. But, in 2005 I went on a mission trip to Uganda, and in the middle of one night, I left my cot and mosquito netting to sit outside and work on my laptop. There was, of course, no one around, but I now believe I became a "glowing" midnight snack for one famished mosquito. When I returned to the States I came down with malaria. I was so sick I couldn't even raise my head. By God's grace I recovered, but something in my body had changed.

Though I never connected the dots, I began to have pain all over my body. It got so bad, at times, I would literally crawl out of bed and then gradually pull my body up to stand. I was in trouble, and openly spoke to my wife about winding up in a wheelchair. Much prayer went up for my healing, but nothing seemed to help.

Then in 2015, I went to a holistic doctor who asked me to make a list of every malady I ever had. When he saw I checked off malaria, he connected it with my aches and pains, and said assuredly, "Oh, I can take care of that!" I thought, "Sure you can, buddy!" But within a week of taking one tiny pill a day, my chronic body aches vanished. I went back to him and said, "I feel great, but need more pills." He chuckled, "No you don't; that's gone!"

**WHAT! Ten years of debilitating pain, gone with seven tiny pills. I can cry even now. God healed me, and used an unlikely person and method to do so, but I give Him every drop and speck of glory. He is my healer!**

Have you ever thought: "There are so many bad things happening in my life, nothing good could ever come out of it?" Maybe this next thought will comfort you. **The good news of the gospel is good enough to cover all of the bad news in your life. As God is bigger than my problems, His plan for my future won't just work for my good, it will make me the person I really would want to be if I were in my right mind and trusted Him completely.**

**SCRIPTURE** *"If we are faithless, he remains faithful—for he cannot deny himself."* *(2Timothy 2:13)*

**PRINCIPLE:**   WE HAVE ALL GIVEN UP TOO SOON, EVEN
THOUGH GOD'S HELP WAS ON THE WAY.

I once led a man to Jesus who, the week before, had put his neck on a railroad track to take his life, and only lifted it just before the train passed in front of him. He was the father of three young children. Jesus said, "In this world you will have tribulation!"[124] He wasn't overstating this. Life is really tough! Then He added, "But...take heart... take courage... cheer up...I have overcome so that you can overcome." "I'm victorious, so you can be victorious!" Those were not empty words. Because Jesus conquered sin and the death sin produces, we can be "...more than conquerors through Him who loved us and gave His life for us."[125]

**I can certainly relate. I often feel like giving up, but I know better, and swat that lie. We all tend to want to give up too soon! What we need to do is wait on God; for the victory behind His promises. If, as the Bible says, "experience gives hope,"[126] have you lived long enough to learn from your experiences, and accepted the fact that being obedient is infinitely better than being impulsive, safe is far more desirable than reckless, and careful always trumps careless?**

All of us are hoping to have a blessed life. But we can never get around the principle of reaping what we sow. There is no bargaining with God. The Bible declares this unbreakable law, "Do not be deceived: God is not mocked, for whatever one sows, that will he also reap. For the one who sows to his own flesh will from the flesh reap corruption, but the one who sows to the Spirit will from the Spirit reap eternal life."[127] **Holy Spirit, help me to obey You, that I may truly live!**

**SCRIPTURE** *"Shadrach, Meshach and Abednego said, '...our God whom we serve is able to deliver us from the burning fiery furnace, and He will deliver us out of your hand, O king. But if not, be it known to you, O king, that we will not serve your gods...'" (Daniel 3:17–18)*

124. JOHN 16:33
125. ROMANS 8:37
126. ROMANS 5:4
127. GALATIANS 6: 7–8
128. PSALM 5:12

# GETTING SUED BUT DOING THE RIGHT THING

**PRINCIPLE:** THE ANSWER TO LIFE'S STRUGGLES IS NEVER "WHY, GOD?" BUT "WHAT, GOD?"

**God never misses an opportunity to make us more like Him. That usually manifests itself in significant challenges. They are the training ground for spiritual maturity.**

A year after we sold our house in 2004, the new owners sued us, claiming they discovered mold in the house, and believed we knew about it. We didn't. But off to arbitration we went. The owners were so upset with us they wouldn't meet in the same room. Word had it that they were questioning our integrity and even our Christian character. **It was a perfect opportunity for God to bring peace and healing to an impossible situation.**

Our room had lawyers, our real estate agent, my wife and I, and the arbitrator. We were presented, for the first time, pictures of the mold behind the walls of the home. It made me sick and sad. I wanted to cry. After discussion with our Christian real estate agent, Brent Gove, our response was immediate and heartfelt. I challenged all of us in the room to do the right thing for this couple, and then looking at the arbitrator said, "I don't believe it is right for us to give the owners what they are asking for. We need to do much more!" The arbitrator just stared at me. Then gathering his thoughts, he said, "I've been doing this for 20 years, and I've never heard anyone say to me what you just did. I believe the owners will be happy to meet you now."

When the owners came in, we both had tears in our eyes. I looked at them and said, "We had no idea!" We then hugged. God had done a marvelous job arbitrating our test.

**Whether I eat dirt or humble pie is always my decision. Humility has been defined as "having or showing a modest or low estimate of one's own importance." No one can humble me. Humility must be my own preference.**

Former prisoner of war under the Nazis, Corrie ten Boom, was once asked if it was difficult for her to remain humble. Her reply was simple, "When Jesus rode into Jerusalem on Palm Sunday on the back of a donkey, and everyone was waving palm branches, throwing garments on the road, and singing praises, do you think that for one moment the donkey thought any of that was for him?"

---

**SCRIPTURE** *"And if anyone would sue you and take your tunic, let him have your cloak as well. And if anyone forces you to go one mile, go with him two miles. Give to the one who begs from you, and do not refuse the one who would borrow from you.'"* (Matthew 5:40–42)

# PRIDEFUL AFTER HEARING A POSITIVE REPORT

**PRINCIPLE:** NEVER UNDERESTIMATE OUR ABILTY TO GET SO VERY EXCITED ABOUT SO VERY LITTLE.

When one of my daughters had a newborn baby, I took the weekend off from our church services to be with her. We spent the morning walking and talking. It was wonderful! But as our time progressed and I received text messages about how well the services were going in my absence, **I found my heart being filled with pride. It was very unsettling. So much so, that by Tuesday when I met with the elders, I confessed it with tears. It scared me! What had caused my heart to be so seduced with self?**

It took me a couple of weeks to solve the mystery, but once I did, it became an important milestone of insight. **Because I had not spoken during the weekend services, I had not been sufficiently humbled by my own inadequacy.** Invariably, I would have said things I wished I hadn't, and that experience of missing the mark would have enabled me to leave the church sufficiently deflated and dependent upon God to make the difference in people's lives. By not speaking and yet hearing good reports, I was basking in the illusion of having done something, when, in reality, I had done nothing to merit the success we were having.

Whether I eat dirt or humble pie is always my decision. Humility has been defined as "having or showing a modest or low estimate of one's own importance." No one can humble me. Humility must be my own preference.

Sir Isaac Newton's first law of motion determined that an object stays in motion as long as no opposing force is put on the object. Winds that are close to the Earth's surface are less intense since friction has reduced their wind speed. **If I humble myself and bow to God, I will be less tossed about by the winds of adversity. Whether I stand proud or bow humbly will most certainly affect my quality of life. I choose to bow to my Creator, for only then can He lift me up above the more unsettling winds of life.**

**SCRIPTURE** *"Pride goes before destruction, and a haughty spirit before a fall."' (Proverbs 16:18) "...when he (the Holy Spirit) comes, he will convict the world concerning sin and righteousness and judgment." (John 16:8)*

# PATIENT OBEDIENCE KEPT US FROM LOSING EVERYTHING

**PRINCIPLE:** ONLY BY OBEYING THE GOD WHO KNOWS THE FUTURE, WILL OUR LIVES BE PROTECTED.

Shortly after selling our home in 2004, we purchased land with the intent to build. A contractor friend offered to build it for slightly above cost. In addition, we received a recommendation to hire a young architect to draw up plans. The house was not elaborate, but for whatever reason our architect just couldn't complete the floor plan. Literally, two years passed. Everyone, and that means everyone, encouraged me to get a new architect. But, after praying much about the decision, I just couldn't get a peace to let him go.

Ultimately, this stalemate went on until the recession of 2007 was in full bloom. Only then did we see why the architect could not finish our plans. Had they been completed, and the financial bottom fell out, we would have lost every penny we had gained from the previous investment. God had stopped us from proceeding. Had we bulldozed our way forward, we would have lost everything.

**Never forget you are not the brains of any operation. That role is reserved for the God who knows all things, but who will guide His beloved children, if we will but wait and ask.** We'd all love to get the inside scoop on a foolproof investment; one that's guaranteed to provide for our future in a significant way. Well, only God offers just such an opportunity. But with a serious caution! Don't "...trust in uncertain riches but in the living God, who gives us richly all things to enjoy."[129] **"He who provides for this life but takes no care for eternity is wise for a moment but a fool forever."[130] That pretty much sums it up. Why appear to be wise chasing riches on this temporary Earth, when you can walk in the wisdom of God that guarantees an incomparable return... forever.**

**SCRIPTURE** *"For you have need of endurance, so that when you have done the will of God you may receive what is promised." (Hebrews 10:36)*

129. 1TIMOTHY 1:17B, NLT
130. JOHN TILLOTSON, ARCHBISHOP OF CANTERBURY

# BROTHER TERESA REACHES CITYWIDE PASTORS

**PRINCIPLE:** GOD CHOOSES VESSELS WHO ARE LIKE HIM TO REPRESENT HIM.

A couple pastoring a small church in our region decided to reach out and encourage other pastors by having a quarterly luncheon consisting of food, fellowship and prayer. Initially, when I and 30 other pastors attended, I was concerned that they couldn't afford to do it. But, in short order, their gracious, humble leadership was so attractive to pastors in need of encouragement that I, and many other leaders, joined them in undergirding and underwriting this region-transforming event. Such was the origin of City Pastors Fellowship in Sacramento, California. Now, each quarter, 400 senior pastors, ministry leaders, and youth and young adult leaders come for food, fellowship and prayer.

We affectionately call Don Proctor, Brother Teresa, because he selflessly reaches across denominational, geographic, and racial divides to love men and woman of God in corporate fellowship. Every month he sends out over 400 personalized texts, affirming and valuing leaders desperately in need of encouragement.

Don and his wife, Christa, personify the main goal of being a Christ-follower: to become like Jesus. The fact is—being like Jesus isn't the pinstripes on a car. It's the engine. Character is not a consolation prize. It's the main event. Romans 8:29 says, that God chose us to become like His Son, so that His Son would be the firstborn among many brothers and sisters. **Our becoming like Jesus is the fulfillment of God's original intention: creating us in the image and likeness of God.**

In 2016, Don and Christa bought a home. Without realizing it, until it was purchased, the house was on the corner of two cross-streets: Unity and Community. A serendipitous affirmation of God's hand on their life, family, and ministry.

**The Bible says, "Don't look out only for your own interests, but take an interest in others, too. You must have the same attitude that Christ Jesus had."[131] Being like Jesus is the fulfillment of being created in God's image; and the fruit of Him being the first fruits of God's new creation. Don't chase after what lasts for only a moment. Pursue what lasts forever...becoming like Jesus; it is the greatest honor in life and the only life worth pursuing.**

**SCRIPTURE** *"But God chose what is foolish in the world to shame the wise; God chose what is weak in the world to shame the strong; then they realized they had been with Jesus." (1Corinthians 1:27) "Now when they saw the boldness of Peter and John, and perceived that they were uneducated, common men, they were astonished. And they recognized that they had been with Jesus." (Acts 4:13)*

131. PHILIPPIANS 2:4–5, NLT

## PRAYING IN CEMETERIES IN SICILY WITH SIBLINGS

**PRINCIPLE:** ONLY BY GOING TO THE ROOT CAN WE SEE TRANSFORMATION IN OUR FRUIT.

My father was born in Sicily, where my mother's parents were born as well. So, in 2008, I and my two brothers, Victor and Joseph, and two sisters, Diana and Maria, went on a spiritual pilgrimage to our ancestral homeland. Since Diana had lived in Rome for over 40 years and knew the language, our trip to Sicily was made easier. All five of us were followers of Jesus for decades, and between us we had 18 children and over 30 grandchildren.

The purpose of our journey, in addition to enjoying each other's company, was to spend a significant amount of time praying over our generational history and future legacy. Since we had each been graced with an extra dose of intensity, delving into the quarries of our ancestral challenges was something we were primed to do. We took a giant four-foot by three-foot sheet of paper and listed every ancestral sin, bondage or deception we could think of...and there was no shortage. We then meticulously prayed over each issue, in hotel rooms, restaurants, and even in the graveyards of the towns in which our parents and grandparents were born. It wasn't spooky, but it was gut-level real! Jesus said, "...the ruler of this world...has no claim on me..."[132] We believe the same for those we love and cover.

**The extraordinary byproduct of this season of focused intercessory prayer for me personally was the fact that I've not had a bad thought about my father since that time.** At the time of our expedition he had been dead 42 years and, for me, having choking thoughts about things he did and didn't do were common. **But I believe two things served to deliver me from these gnawing reflections: the intercessory mission to Sicily with my siblings and during the six months prior to the journey, writing a book entitled, "Father Wounds," which included as much journaling about my own father issues as writing for others.**

**So, let me leave you with this final question. What open portals of ancestral sin, bondage, and deception continue to affect you and those you love? Let the blood of Jesus cover, deliver and protect both you and them.**

---

**SCRIPTURE** *"Keeping steadfast love for thousands, forgiving iniquity and transgression and sin, but who will by no means clear the guilty, visiting the iniquity of the fathers on the children and the children's children, to the third and the fourth generation." (Exodus 34:7)*

132. JOHN 14:30

# THE ONE PERSON I WANT TO SEE IN HEAVEN

2008

**PRINCIPLE:** THE PERSON WHO HURT YOU THE MOST JUST MIGHT BE THE KEY TO YOUR GREATEST HEALING.

No one hurt me more on Earth than my father. Growing up, he was the angriest man I knew, and the person I least wanted to see. He never visited a boarding school I attended, and in 1966 when I was 17 years old, two hours before he died suddenly of a massive heart attack, I said to my twin brother Joseph, "I wish he would drop dead!"

It is crushing to even write this. Yet, as I wrote in the dedication of my book "Father Wounds" in 2008, "To my earthly father: Though you are the person who hurt me most on earth, you are the one I long to see most in heaven. May our heavenly Father grant that we meet again as healed brothers in Christ. Your son, Francis"

The Bible says, "...the glory of children is their fathers."[133] "Glory" here refers to an "ornament worn around the neck." It is a showpiece, something to be proud of. We all want to honor our fathers. This statement is not offered as a possibility. It is presented as a fact. Deep down we want to say, "My Dad's better than your Dad!" Sadly, few of us really believe this.

Everyone's important to God. We're all created in His image and likeness—given precious deposits of His character, personality and gifting. Therefore, everyone should be important to us—and treated with respect. Since God believes in honoring, it should be one of our premiere values as well.

**The Bible says, "Honor all people."[134] This word "honor" literally means, "to prize, to revere, to value." Often prejudice comes from lack of honor and respect. We devalue someone else for our own benefit. Honoring and respecting others would completely eliminate prejudice from the planet. But though we honor others, we should never take honor away from God. Likewise, we must never focus on receiving honor for ourselves. In that way, honor is like chewing gum. Enjoy it briefly, but don't swallow it.**

**SCRIPTURE** *"Be kind to one another, tenderhearted, forgiving one another, as God in Christ forgave you." (Ephesians 4:32)*

133. PROVERBS 17:6
134. 1PETER 2:17, NKJV

# THE
# SACRAMENTO
*2000–2013* YEARS

# THE SACRAMENTO YEARS

*2000–2013*

SACRAMENTO CITY PASTOR'S FELLOWSHIP QUARTERLY LUNCHEON

Pastor

Police Chief

PASTOR LES SIMMONS AND SAC POLICE CHIEF SAM SOMERS

G-KIDS RISING

MY DEAR SISTER, DR. JOY JOHNSON

FILMING IN WALES WITH JOEL & SUZIE

OUR FAMILY ON VACATION

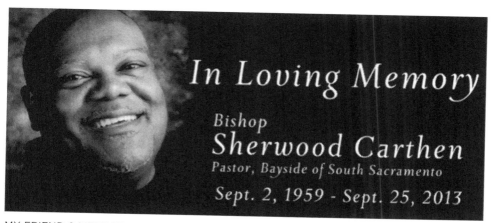

*In Loving Memory*

Bishop
**Sherwood Carthen**
Pastor, Bayside of South Sacramento

Sept. 2, 1959 - Sept. 25, 2013

MY FRIEND & MENTOR, BISHOP SHERWOOD CARTHEN

ROSEVILLE POLICE CHIEF DANIEL HAHN

MY BEST FRIEND, SUZIE

# "SACRAMENTO" PUTS A NEW DOOR IN OUR HOME

**PRINCIPLE:** GOD WANTS TO COMMISSION YOU TO DO HIS WILL. SO, BE EVER WATCHFUL!

In 2009, Suzie and I hired a man from an online handyman service to put a new door in our home. When he introduced himself and said his name was "Sacramento", my heart froze. God had been actively speaking to me about my further involvement with Sacramento leaders, and this came as a confirmation. Sacramento was putting a new door in my life.

Within a year we had placed Bob Hasty, a dear friend for 25 years, as a co-senior pastor of our home church, The Rock of Roseville. That structural adjustment enabled me to divide my time and focus between the Rock and the Region. God further affirmed prophetically that as I was a twin, and had twin, so my energies were to be equally divided between the Rock and the Region. God's wisdom proved to be both effective and fruitful.

Did I feel capable? Absolutely not! But, that's actually a healthy place to be: having no confidence in my own ability—realizing if I rely on my own efforts I cannot become who God has asked me to be, nor do what He's asked me to do. When David was living in a cave, as an outcast, he had little choice but to fully trust in God. But when he became a successful king, he counted his army and relied on his own strength.[135] **Rejoice in your weakness, it is your only hope of true success. "For when I am weak, then I am strong."[136]**

Revelations from God are never birthed in time and space, but bloom forever in Heaven. I have had many lesser thoughts that have a shelf life of nanoseconds, but the God-inspired revelations that came as lightning bolts of truth, these are the thoughts I will cherish throughout eternity. The Bible says, "Forever, O Lord, Your word is settled in heaven."[137] "Oh, how I love your instructions! I think about them all day long."[138]

**We will cherish revelations from God forever, because the Word that had no beginning will likewise have no end. The Word that became flesh and walked among us is even now seated on the very Throne of God. It is this eternal Word that reaches out to enlighten us each and every day. God speak! We are desperate to hear You.**

---

**SCRIPTURE** *"...a wide door for effective work has opened to me..." (1Corinthians 16:9)*

135. 2SAMUEL 24
136. 2CORINTHIANS 12:10
137. PSALM 119:89, NKJV
138. PSALM 119:97, NLT

OBEDIENCE THAT
COSTS DEARLY

**PRINCIPLE:** AT TIMES, THE LAST THING YOU WANT
TO DO IS THE FIRST THING YOU MUST DO.

I was good friends with a national Christian leader who asked my counsel about a very serious decision he was making. My desire was only to help, but my advice was the opposite of what others had encouraged him to do. The situation became quite tense between us. Because I believed so strongly things would end badly for my friend, my appeal increased in intensity, but to no avail. It strained our friendship. I had mixed feelings, but believed I'd done the right thing, though it cost me dearly, and it didn't alter his decision.

Over time, the effects of his decision were realized. It was very sad. Ultimately, we were reconciled with tears, and he acknowledged, "I should have followed your advice; it would have saved me a lot of pain."

The Bible says, "Faithful are the wounds of a friend, But the kisses of an enemy are deceitful." There are decisions we make in life that may be right, but the consequences may feel so wrong, we wonder if we would do it again. I've never felt good about how it all transpired. It still makes me sad. But, I was left with only one option: do the right thing to help a friend, or take the easy road and just agree with the "bad" counsel of others.

**It is estimated that 45 million Christ-followers have given their lives as martyrs since the birth of the Church in the first century. They died obediently following Jesus, but going against the crowd cost them much. But not everything.**

**In eternity we will see the sacrifices we've made on Earth will pale in comparison with the reward we will receive. "For I consider that the sufferings of this present time are not worth comparing with the glory that is to be revealed to us."[140] The price of obedience is the best investment we will ever make.**

**SCRIPTURE** *"...to them we did not yield in submission even for a moment, so that the truth of the gospel might be preserved for you. And from those who seemed to be influential (what they were makes no difference to me; God shows no partiality)..."*
*Galatians 2:5–6a*

139. PROVERBS 27:6, NKJV
140. ROMANS 8:18

**PRINCIPLE:** YOU WILL BE SURPRISED AT SOME OF THE FRIENDSHIPS GOD HAS PREPARED FOR YOU.

I was once invited to a luncheon for about 50 leaders at a small Hispanic church in our city. There were people from many races, but I was the only Caucasian in the room. At the end of the meeting, an anointed African-American leader, Dr. Joy Johnson, was asked to briefly share and pray. I was so captivated by the grace on her life that when she finished, I made a beeline for her. The more questions I asked, the more I was drawn to her ministry.

I then had my personal assistant contact her and set up an appointment to find out more about the 2,000-person, low-income, apartment complex she and her team had turned "right-side up." Little did I know that this person I met in 2009 would become such a close friend and strategic regional partner.

It took a while for Joy to share the backstory of our first meeting, but eventually it leaked out. **While she was the first person in the room I wanted to meet, I was the last she wanted to talk to.** As the token "white guy," she didn't know my motive for being there, and assumed, as she says now with a chuckle, "I figured you were just there to pick up the check, and so when I prayed, I was praying for everyone but you."

Since then, in the marvelous plan of God, we've had many luncheons together, and she has spoken at our church a number of times, all of which have led to numerous encounters of racial unity. On one of those anointed occasions, God led me, with tears, to publically wash her feet. With our spouses at our sides, Joy felt a release from the pain of prejudice she had repeatedly experienced due to her race, and even a healing from being rejected by male leaders who considered her a threat because she is a powerful woman in ministry.

**Dr. Joy Johnson is now universally recognized as a mighty, respected regional leader, and she is one of my closest friends in ministry. We have teamed up to see the Kingdom of God expand. But it all started in the most unlikely of ways, with a chasm that Jesus longed to heal and use as a catalyst for good.**

Who is God going to lead you to heal a breach for and build a lasting friendship with?

**SCRIPTURE** *"And your ancient ruins shall be rebuilt; you shall raise up the foundations of many generations; you shall be called the repairer of the breach, the restorer of streets to dwell in." (Isaiah 58:12)*

# FIGHTING NUMBNESS

**PRINCIPLE:** SOME OF THE THINGS WE BELIEVE ARE KEEPING US ALIVE ARE, INSTEAD, KILLING US.

I may be going numb, but I refuse to go quietly! Every day I fight to stay awake, to "...strengthen what remains and is about to die." I believe God fights with me. Ours is the age of little discernment, the wild west of moral ambiguity, where most people do what's right in their own eyes.

Without the biblical compass of good and evil, truth and lies, who determines what's right and wrong? Without divine discernment, we choose if babies live or die. We determine if selling their body parts is right or wrong. We decide what our eyes should see and what our hearts should embrace. We determine our gender, who we give ourselves to physically, and what defines a marriage. We even believe we get to choose when we die. **In the end, we become counterfeit creators, created in the image of our vain imaginations, putting our hope in what can never fulfill or come to pass.**

Compare Noah Webster's 1828 American Dictionary definition of the word "discern." He wrote, "to see or understand the difference...between good and evil, truth and falsehood." What a tremendous definition! Unfortunately, modern editors corrupted it. **The 2015 version of the Merriam-Webster Dictionary defines discern: "to recognize or identify right from wrong." No longer is it "to see or understand the difference ...between good and evil, truth and falsehood." With good and evil, and truth and lies removed, we're left with mere personal preference, and nothing resembling absolute truth. Ironically, this new and improved definition of "discern" completely lacks discernment.**

**Jesus admonishes each of us, "See that no one leads you astray."**[142] There's nothing more dangerous than a partial truth, because a complete lie is rarely believable. So, when the devil tempted Adam and Eve and said, if you eat of the Tree of the Knowledge of Good and Evil, "...God knows that your eyes will be opened..."[143], they believed him. Their eyes were opened all right, but all they could see was a tsunami of shame hurtling toward them.[144] They realized that, without God, when our "eyes are opened" we see less, not more. I did drugs. My eyes were opened. I saw less. I disobeyed my conscience... my eyes were opened. I saw less. Disobedience always brings shame, and we see less not more. Follow God's warnings, for they always lead to a safe and healthy future.

**SCRIPTURE** *"But the one who hears and does not do them is like a man who built a house on the ground without a foundation. When the stream broke against it, immediately it fell, and the ruin of that house was great." (Luke 6:49)*

141. REVELATION 3:2
142. MATTHEW 24:4
143. GENESIS 3:5
144. GENESIS 3:7

**PRINCIPLE:** IT IS ONLY BY ALLOWING GOD TO EMPTY US, THAT WE CAN BE FILLED.

**The more I know me, the less impressed I am. That's not an overstatement.**

If, as Jesus said, "...he who is forgiven little, loves little,"[145] why would I want to diminish what He did on the cross by inflating who I am? Jesus suffered a horrible death to rescue me, and I never want to take that for granted by minimizing my sin. God loves me with His unconditional, "in spite of" love, and uses me notwithstanding my shortcomings.

So the fact that, since 2011, I am one of the few people privileged to deliver one-minute devotionals every day on K-LOVE Christian Radio to millions of listeners boggles my mind. I regularly receive encouragements from people I will never meet on Earth who have been strengthened by something I've shared. Perhaps I am given the opportunity of offering hope to the hopeless, and courage to the discouraged, because I am so acutely aware of my own humanity and frailty.

Yet, regardless of what I am not, I firmly believe that God doesn't make junk! Everything He has created is remarkable, exceptional and one-of-a-kind. From snowflakes to sunflowers, elephants to ants, penguins to people, God's creation is amazing.

**The devil tries to destroy the extraordinariness of our lives, just like he destroyed his own. But don't give up the riches of Heaven for the counterfeit treasures of Earth. Jesus said, "...the kingdom of heaven is like a merchant seeking beautiful pearls, who, when he had found one pearl of great price, went and sold all that he had and bought it."[146] I used to read this and think, "I need to give God my whole heart in order to get the pearl of great price... Jesus."**

**Now, I realize, God is the merchant and we are His pearls. He gave everything He had for us, even His life, so that we can fulfill His marvelous identity and destiny for us, both here on Earth and throughout eternity.**

---

**SCRIPTURE** *"And Samuel said (to Saul), 'Though you are little in your own eyes, are you not the head of the tribes of Israel? The Lord anointed you king over Israel.'" 1Samuel 15:17*

145. LUKE 7:47
146. MATTHEW 13:45-46, NKJV

**PRINCIPLE:** OBEYING THE UNIQUE CALL ON YOUR LIFE WILL BRING YOU CLOSER TO JESUS.

The call of God on each of our lives is personal. Superimposing what He has asked me to do on others will always end badly. Therefore, let me share candidly, God has asked me to fast often.[147] It has been a key, fine-tuning discipline, forcing me to see myself, as I really am—frail and needy. But likewise to see Jesus as humble and obedient.

When I fast, and by that I mean, I give up some pleasure for a season whether it be food or entertainment. I don't fast because I think I'm super-spiritual; I fast because I know I'm not. Fasting doesn't bring out the best in me; it often exposes the worst. Spiritual toxins bloat and constipate my relationship with God. It is only when I allow the Spirit and the Word to wash over my soul that I am cleansed.[148] Like Job, I confess my desperate need for God's Word, "I have treasured the words of His mouth more than my necessary food."[149]

In Matthew 4, Jesus was led by the Holy Spirit to go into the wilderness to be tempted by Satan. He fasted 40 days and nights. Then "...the tempter came to Him, he said, 'If You are the Son of God, command that these stones become bread.' But Jesus answered and said, 'It is written, "Man shall not live by bread alone, but by every word that proceeds from the mouth of God.' "[150] **Jesus needed the humility of fasting to activate the raw power of the Word of God. Masses of humanity gorge themselves on the crumbs of Earth; not realizing their true hunger is for the feasts of Heaven.**

Many years ago, when safes had rotary combination locks, thieves would use their fingers as hypersensitive listening devices. The most astute safecrackers would file the calluses off their fingertips to become more sensitive to the slightest gyrations of the lock. **In fasting, we file away the hardness of life, in order to hear the still, small voice of our Creator.** We were each created to get to know God. When distractions are eliminated; true feasting begins.

**SCRIPTURE** *"Jesus told His startled disciples, "I have food to eat of which you do not know," (John 4:32) "My food is to do the will of Him who sent Me, and to finish His work." (John 4:34)*

147. 2CORINTHIANS 11:27, 2CORINTHIANS 6:5
148. INSIGHTS ON THE VALUE OF FASTING AT FRANCISANFUSO.COM/FASTING
149. JOB 23:12, NKJV
150. MATTHEW 4:3-4

**PRINCIPLE:** SINCE GOD IS THE GOD OF HAPPY ENDINGS, THERE WILL BE NO REGRETS IN HEAVEN.

If you are hurting from the pain of abortion, I understand how you feel. I myself had two abortions before I met Jesus, and though I have two beautiful daughters, I have no sons. I am so grateful that I have been forgiven and have experienced much healing in this area.

**Years ago, when I accepted the fact that I would see these children in Heaven, I realized I could not refer to them any longer as Abortion One and Abortion Two.** It was then that God showed me my lost children were sons and even gave me names for them: Noah and Caleb.

One day my wife and I were on a hike with two of our grandchildren in the majestic Sequoias of Northern California. That day we had received word that a dear couple in our church had a recent abortion. I was crushed. For many years I had openly talked about the pain and foolishness of my abortions, and so was mystified that someone in our church family could make such a choice. Even though the day was beautiful with the sun glistening off the largest living things on Earth, my heart was broken.

Since our walk was in the snowy off-season, no one was on the trail. Suddenly, we ran into a couple with two small boys. Trying to get out of my emotional funk, I struck up a conversation and found out the boys' names. You guessed it, Noah and Caleb. **It was a miracle. Coming at just the right moment. God had affirmed once again, that in eternity we will see the children we have lost on Earth.**

Are you lamenting an abortion? **My heart aches for you, because God aches for you. Not over the sin, but because he grieves for you to receive His complete forgiveness, and to begin the healing process of rejecting denial, and acknowledging that God's forgiving grace is sufficient to wash away all sin.** "If we confess our sins, he is faithful and just to forgive us our sins and to cleanse us from all unrighteousness."[151]

**SCRIPTURE** *""See that you do not despise one of these little ones. For I tell you that in heaven their angels always see the face of my Father who is in heaven." (Matthew 18:10)*

151. 1JOHN 1:9

# GOD TOLD ME, "YOU'RE NOT SAFE!"

**PRINCIPLE:** TAKE HEED TO THE WARNINGS OF THE HOLY SPIRIT. NONE ARE ACCIDENTAL.

Having been saved in a revival in 1972 called the Jesus Movement, primarily because of the prayers of my mother, I have a special affinity and burden to see a mighty move of God again. Consequently, I have read and written books on revivals, and about the great revivalists and evangelists who helped spearhead them.

In June of 2011, I was particularly burdened about the deteriorating condition of our culture and the evident lack of spiritual passion within much of the church. Going away for a few days to pray and fast about this concern led me to return with convictions to do long fasts, write books and produce videos, all with the intent of jumpstarting the church to reach the lost. About six months into these efforts, the Holy Spirit spoke clearly to me, "You're not safe!" In other words, you know the inherent dangers of pursuing this effort, but you don't have enough spiritual protection to keep you and your family safe. It scared me!

I was soon led, in tears, to ask some of the faithful intercessors I knew for help. God then provided a prayer strategy and structure to keep both them and me safe. But, one week after commissioning 15 intercessors to pray for me, five key individuals I knew well were attacked. One had his son die in his arms of a gunshot wound, two others had their marriages collapse into divorce, and the final two were rocked to their core. This brought about the immediate realization that every leader I knew needed an intercessory team praying for them. During the past five years in our region, over 750 intercessors from 150 churches have now been trained to intercede for their pastors and spiritual leaders.

**Until I was desperate enough to ask, even beg others to pray for me, I felt vulnerable... unsafe. I needed to be honest with those closest to me. I now believe the day I cease being willing to share my vulnerabilities and ask for prayer is the day my safe and abundant Christian life is in serious jeopardy. I want to finish well and complete the mission God has given me, but unless I am willing to pursue the protective measures God provides, more may be lost than gained.**

**SCRIPTURE** *"Put on the whole armor of God, that you may be able to stand against the schemes of the devil." (Ephesians 6:11)*

# OF INTERCESSORS AND ARMOR BEARERS

**PRINCIPLE:** WE ALL NEED TO PRAY FOR THE PROTECTION OF OTHERS, AND FOR OTHERS TO PRAY FOR US.

I know what it's like to be in grave danger; for my life to hang by a thread. I'll never forget the fragility of my past and how many I've known who have seen their lives sabotaged by poor decisions or lack of spiritual protection. We all have too much to lose, but I am particularly conscious of what I have been blessed with, and how tragic it would be to suffer an unnecessary loss of health, family, friends, or ministry. Consequently, I cannot begin to describe how essential intercessors and armor bearers are in order for this not to happen.

In biblical times, an armor bearer was someone who carried the protective gear, armor, and weapons of a warrior. The physical protection they provided is comparable to the spiritual safeguarding needed in our age. Since January of 2012, fifteen intercessors have been consistently praying for physical, emotional and spiritual protection, for my family and myself. I meet regularly with these men and women about my prayer needs, and even the struggles and temptations I face. Additionally, we communicate via voice memos, emails and texts. These faithful prayer warriors fast, pray, and willingly intercede for, not just my family's needs, but also for the stewardship and vision God has given to me. I would attribute many of the miraculous breakthroughs we have experienced to their intercession.

How about you? Are you praying for the needs of others? Have you likewise enlisted others to pray for you? If you were in trouble, would there be anyone who could speak into your life? All of us need people who can do this! **Though none of us want to be controlled, we should all see our need for spiritual accountability. Control is deciding what people can and can't do. Accountability is giving an account of what a person has or has not already done. Control is more of a power issue. Accountability is an issue of integrity. Every one of us need people who can speak into our lives; to pray for us, to hold our feet to the fire, to provoke us to do the right thing, and even to believe with us for the impossible!**

**SCRIPTURE** *The Apostle Paul wrote, "Luke alone is with me." (2Timothy 4:11) Biblical Armor Bearers: 1Samuel 10:26, 16:21, 2Samuel 18:15; Jesus was the ultimate Armor Bearer: Luke 6:12-13*

# "WHEN ARE YOU GOING TO COME TO US?"

**PRINCIPLE:** CARING FOR WOUNDED HEARTS WILL OPEN DOORS OF OPPORTUNITY AND DESTINY.

I once went on a prayer retreat with pastors from the Sacramento region. One of them, Bishop Sherwood Carthen, was a leading African-American pastor. He was greatly esteemed by leaders in both the church community and secular culture, and had been the chaplain of the Sacramento Kings basketball team for over a decade.

One afternoon, a very candid discussion took place about race realities between Sherwood and another highly respected white pastor. I stayed out of the discussion until I felt they were at an impasse. They both loved and respected each other, but somehow they just weren't connecting. Finally, with great emotion, I said to Sherwood, "My brother, what do you want us to do? We'll do whatever you ask."

**He expressed that there seemed to be little effort, amongst many church leaders, to build bridges of understanding and healing. He then added a knockout sentence. "The road from me to you is the same distance as from you to me. We are always coming to you. When are you going to come to us?" The words were piercing to all of us! With a second chance to hear Sherwood's heart, he was finally heard.**

Further discussion of specifics brought about City Pastors Fellowship involvement in future events connecting us with the African-American community in our region, one of which is the annual "MLK – March For The Dream" which takes place every January. Within a year, hundreds of pastors, leaders and believers from throughout our region marched in support with thousands of our African-American brothers and sisters. Many pastors and leaders of all races now march every year, and I believe there will even be an increased involvement from pastors and churches in years to come.

All of this was a result of that one awkward, yet vulnerable conversation. Which leads me to share a vitally important conviction. **The church and the culture really need faithful, godly, servant leaders...willing to ask, hear, and respond to uncomfortable and troublesome questions.**

**Will you be one of those leaders? At times, we have to hate what we have become in order to embrace what we are meant to be. It will take courage to be a rescuer in this age of rampant numbness! It will take even more courage to first reject numbness in ourselves.** The Bible says, "God has not given us a spirit of fear and timidity, but of power, love, and self-discipline."[152]

---

**SCRIPTURE** *"And a vision appeared to Paul in the night: a man of Macedonia was standing there, urging him and saying, 'Come over to Macedonia and help us.'" (Acts 16:9)*

152. 2TIMOTHY 1:7, NKJV

# MIRACLES WHILE FILMING THE WELSH REVIVAL

**PRINCIPLE:** GOD LOVES TO DO MIRACLES TO AFFIRM HE IS THE AUTHOR.

In 2012, my wife, Suzie, and I and a videographer, Joel Sandvos, flew from California to the nation of Wales to film in the actual locations where the Welsh Revival of 1904 took place.[153] But as our plane left the ground, we had not yet secured final permission to film in the main location, Moriah Chapel. Fighting for a breakthrough, a team of faithful intercessors stayed up and prayed all night. Permission came as we arrived.

Also, weather in Wales during the timeframe we were filming would typically be rainy but, as God would have it, we had so many days of continual sun, we had to buy suntan lotion. I actually got sunburned. Two weeks after filming on a creek bed in one of our locations, the ground was completely covered by torrential rains and a river of water. Our success was always in God's hands, but it still required trusting Him more than the impossibilities we were facing. The Bible declares, "Now faith is the substance of the things we are hoping for, and the evidence of the things we cannot yet see."[154]

**God's love is unconditional, but accessing His life and grace always requires conditional faith.** The Bible says, "Just as the body is dead without breath, so also faith is dead without good works."[155] This principle was evident even in the Old Testament story about Naaman, the Syrian general. He would not have been healed of his leprosy if he had been unwilling to obey God, speaking through the prophet Elijah, to dip in the Jordan River seven times.

**So, yes, God's love is unconditional; it is freely given to each of us. In order to receive this marvelous love, we're going to have to step out in conditional faith. This will take effort, obedience, and often, great courage. But, the reward of walking in this level of faith is joining us in a miraculous way with the God of the supernatural.**

**SCRIPTURE** *"By faith the people crossed the Red Sea as on dry land, but the Egyptians, when they attempted to do the same, were drowned." (Hebrews 11:29) "And he (Jesus) awoke and rebuked the wind and said to the sea, 'Peace! Be still!' And the wind ceased, and there was a great calm." (Mark 4:39)*

153. VIDEO LINK: WWW.REVIVALSTORIES.ORG/?P=396
154. HEBREWS 11:1-2
155. JAMES 2:26, NLT

# STAYING IN THE HOME OF A GREAT REVIVALIST

**PRINCIPLE:** WHEN WE DIG IN THE WELLS OF PAST GIANTS, WE FIND KEYS TO THE SUPERNATURAL.

Of the handful of nation-transforming revivals that have taken place since Pentecost and the birth of the church, many consider the Welsh revival of 1904 the most Earth-shaking and Heaven summoning. It came, as revivals invariably do, during a low-tide spiritual moment. Empty churches, cold hearts, lethargic Christians, and flourishing evil. Up steps a 27-year-old coal miner named Evan Roberts, eager to see God move as He did in the beginning of creation: "...and darkness was upon the face of the deep. And the Spirit of God moved upon the face of the waters."[156]

Our journey to film in the nation of Wales in May of 2012 was both earth shaking and paradigm shifting. We were exhausted most of the time, suffering from jet lag, filming take after take, and driving to what seemed like an infinite number of locations. One night, Suzie and I stayed in Island House, Evan Roberts' childhood home, and even slept in the very room he experienced nightly visitations with Jesus, over a period of three months. To say the least, we were overjoyed to be in such a special place. So, when I got up early to seek the Lord as I always do, my heart was filled with anticipation. This was where Evan Roberts communed with Jesus, and I wanted any impartation or insight God would give me.

Evan grew up in a family of eight children, with two dying in childhood. Originally, the back of the house had a ladder going up to a loft, where, as it was described, children were stacked like cord wood. So, the environment was busy and noisy. Not the ideal place for quiet reflection, but perfect for God to visit Evan in the middle of the night.

**As I prayed and reflected early that morning, I received just one clear thought that I believe, in some way, describes Evan's entire life journey. The Holy Spirit spoke to my heart, "The Kingdom of God is Within You"[157] There it is! Evan Roberts found an extraordinary connection with Jesus as he opened his spirit. Perhaps there is no clearer explanation to why God used him so mightily. Jesus, move upon our hearts to take us out of darkness, into Your marvelous light!**

**SCRIPTURE** *"...darkness was over the face of the deep. And the Spirit of God was hovering over the face of the waters. And God said..." (Genesis 1:2b–3a)*

156. GENESIS 1:2
157. LUKE 17:21, NKJV

# 2ND AND 3RD HOLES-IN-ONE

---

**PRINCIPLE:** GOD LOVES TO DO MIRACLES TO AFFIRM HE IS THE AUTHOR.

---

While my 1st hole-in-one was significant in getting my attention, my 2nd and 3rd, occurring just a few weeks apart, were even more impacting.

During the early winter of 2013, I was particularly burdened about our need for movement in the Spirit realm related to revival. Fasting, praying, and getting up early to seek God are a regular part of my spiritual disciplines. But, I still needed to get out of my intense focus on our desperate need for revival, and enjoy some exercise, fellowship, and fun. Though I am not a good golfer, it provides a perfect environment for these three objectives.

On November 7, 2013, I made my 2nd hole-in-one ever, and immediately knew it had significance.[158] This was followed, six-weeks and 66 holes later, by another hole-in-one.[159] We calculated the probability of this happening as 1 in 40 million. And if you saw me play you would add a few more zeroes. Again, I was dumbfounded, but fueled by a deep and abiding passion for God to supernaturally move to revive the church in order to awaken the lost. Why do we need a revival? Because a revival does what only God can do. Revival is when God springs a convicting surprise on His creation.

**Unless the church in America changes quickly, we may soon find empty churches standing as reminders of greater days when God once had His way. Unless we pray for, love, reach out to, teach and train the next generation of young people, there may not be a new generation of whole-hearted followers of Jesus in America. Unless we recognize the need to fall on our faces before a holy God and re-pent of our compromise and coldness of heart, we will miss our last best opportunity to see God once again transform families, churches and our nation. God's calling us! Can you sense it? He's drawing us into a deeper place than we've ever been before. Respond to His voice and begin to walk confidently in your future with Him.**

---

**SCRIPTURE** *"...the Lord worked with them and confirmed the message by accompanying signs." (Mark 16:20)*

158. VIDEO LINK: HTTP://TINYURL.COM/HZYJR36
159. VIDEO LINK: HTTP://TINYURL.COM/Z6S9XWU

# THE INTERCESSORY YEARS

*2013–beyond*

# THE INTERCESSORY
*2013–beyond* YEARS

THREE SUPERNATURAL HOLES-IN-ONE

GRANDPA & GRANDSON, BECKHAM

REVIVAL IS A MARATHON

GRANDCHILDREN: L TO R: WESLEY, GABRIELLA, WILLIAM, BECKHAM, JUDAH, & HUDSON

ENJOYING OUR LATER YEARS

THE GREAT MOTHER PRAYING OVER ME

MY PRECIOUS INTERCESSORS PRAYING OVER ME

THE TREE OF OUR GENERATIONAL LEGACY

CORNER OF UNITY & COMMUNITY

# THE LEADER WHO MOST IMPACTED MY YOUTH

**PRINCIPLE:** GOD HAS ALWAYS CHOSEN UNLIKELY VESSELS TO CHANGE THE WORLD.

No leader had a greater impact in my youth than Dr. Martin Luther King Jr. No words are sufficient to express the courage and wisdom I saw in him. He led the civil rights movement for 13 years. During that time, more progress was made for African-Americans to achieve racial equality than in the previous 350 years. Somehow, the pure abandon of his life cut through both the national dysfunction and my own personal confusion. A flawed man, like each of us and nearly every Bible hero, Dr. King remains a champion of truth and conviction. He wrote, "To be a Christian without prayer is no more possible than to be alive without breathing." **He prayed, "Use me, God. Show me how to take who I am, who I want to be, and what I can do, and use it for a purpose greater than myself."**

During the time of Jesus, Samaritans were considered half-breeds, and universally despised by both Jews and Romans. Being Jewish and from Galilee, Jesus had experienced racial prejudice firsthand. He understood the cruelty of discrimination. Consequently, when He was traveling from Judea back home to Galilee, Jesus made a conscious decision not to skirt the prejudice around Him, and faced it head on. He deliberately went through Samaria. A direct route from Judea to Galilee was about 70 miles, or a two-and-a-half-day walk. But, due to prejudice, many Jews were willing to journey about twice the distance on a hotter and more uncomfortable road, rather than go through Samaria. **Jesus cut through this narrow-minded bigotry and many Samaritans from a village named Sachar believed in Him.**[160] **What Samaria is God asking you to go to?**

After the exhortation of Bishop Sherwood Carthen to venture toward the African-American community, I was invited to be part of the MLK Committee that hosts the annual MLK Celebration, which draws thousands to an evening of worship, preaching and honoring recipients of various awards that in some way fulfilled the dream of Dr. King. In addition, I connected with the leaders of the MLK "March For The Dream," the largest of its kind in America. **Building bridges, uniting believers, and healing breaches were a vital part of Christ's ministry. So, now it must be a part of ours.**

---

**SCRIPTURE** *"Jesus taught a parable, 'And the King will answer them, "Truly, I say to you, as you did it to one of the least of these my brothers, you did it to me.'" "* (Matthew 25:40)

160. JOHN 4:39

# MY BEST FRIEND'S MORAL FAILURE

---

**PRINCIPLE:** AS GOD HAS NEVER GIVEN UP ON US,
WE MUST NEVER GIVE UP ON OTHER PEOPLE.

---

On the day I finished preaching a message about the biblical patriarch, King David, entitled, "David, The Great Repenter," I came home to find my wife trembling in the kitchen with her cell phone in hand. She had just received a text from the wife of one of my best friends in ministry, David Loveless. He had just confessed to his wife that he had committed adultery.

This began days, weeks, months, and now years of helping our dear friends recover from the greatest devastation in their life. It was agonizing for them and excruciating for many who watched both near and far. It was so traumatic; there are physical places on this planet that I cannot go to without being taken back to seemingly hopeless phone calls, drowning in tears and despair. Even now, it's hard to think about how dark it was.

But, God's Word is greater than our experiences, "I have never seen the righteous forsaken..."[161] **David and Caron Loveless didn't just recover; their marriage went to a level they had never known, and the insights God showed them have brought healing revelation to thousands, with many more to come. Our friends are back, and my heart weeps for joy!**[162]

Many years before, David had asked me this question twice, "How are you doing?" during a very difficult season in my own life. I was not doing well and broke down in tears. His sincerity and depth of friendship helped me greatly during that trying time. **I will always be indebted to my friend David.**

So, let me ask, "When does a parent cease to be responsible to care about their children? When does a friend stop sharing the truth with a friend?" Never! One of the great lies the devil spreads is, "It's their life! Who am I to tell them how to live?" You're their friend! You're their parent, their brother, their sister—you're the person who's supposed to try and keep them from destroying their lives!

There's a big difference between meddling and protecting. Faithful are the challenges of a friend, but the person who applauds everything you do is not your true friend.[163] It takes courage to speak the truth in love. A friend will tell you what you need to hear, not what you want to hear. Who in your life is waiting for you to be their true friend? It's been said, "In prosperity our friends know us. But, in adversity we know our friends."

---

**SCRIPTURE** *"If anyone is caught in any transgression, you who are spiritual should restore him in a spirit of gentleness. Keep watch on yourself, lest you too be tempted. Bear one another's burdens, and so fulfill the law of Christ." (Galatians 6:1-2)*

161. PSALM 37:25
162. YOULIVETRUE.COM—DAVID AND CARON LOVELESS' MINISTRY
163. PROVERBS 27:6

MEETING SACRAMENTO
FOUNDER'S DESCENDANT

**PRINCIPLE:** GOD ORCHESTRATES MIRACULOUS ENCOUNTERS ALONG THE WAY TO AFFIRM WE ARE HEADING IN THE RIGHT DIRECTION.

**Never believe God doesn't care about little things. Actually, everything compared to Him is a "little thing." But, I believe we each should look for God to speak to us, every day in the little things. Little kisses from God create some of the best memories.**

In the fall of 2014, I went away to fast, pray, and write a script for a video we were producing on, "The Spiritual History of Sacramento".[164] Sacramento's history is actually quite profound. Her original pastors were instrumental in keeping California, when it was founded in 1850, from becoming a slave state.

I was staying at a YWAM (Youth With A Mission) base in Chico, California where, in November of 1972, I had been ordained an Evangelist. I had just finished writing the script and after my computer read it back to me, I was leaving my cabin to go on a prayer walk. Much to my surprise, I ran into the man staying next door whose name was Kevin Sutter, one of the few descendants of the founder of Sacramento, John Sutter.[165] I was blown away! What a sweet encouragement! God knew I needed it.

Even though I know I catch a few of the amazing nuances of God, I'm sure I miss many others as well. Once, as I was getting off a plane to go to a connecting flight, I glanced at the electronic Departure Board to see what gate was next. Having flown so much, I was confident I knew what I was doing. Taking the tram in this busy airport, I arrived at the gate only to realize I had read the flight information incorrectly and actually needed to go back to the original gate I had arrived at 15 minutes before. After racing to get there, I walked back into my first plane and even was assigned the exact same seat. As I sat back, now sweating, 30 minutes into my circular journey, I laughed at my foolishness. God gently reminded me to pay attention, and to not take even little things for granted. It was a good lesson I hope I never forget.

**SCRIPTURE** *"The steps of a [good and righteous] man are directed and established by the Lord, And He delights in his way [and blesses his path]." (Psalm 37:23, Amplified Bible)*

164. VIDEO LINK: HTTP://TINYURL.COM/ZYZBPA8
165. VIDEO LINK: HTTP://TINYURL.COM/J5BEUKO

# SECRETARIAT & FRANCIS BARTLEMAN ANOINTINGS

**PRINCIPLE:** WE ARE CALLED TO FILL THE SHOES OF THOSE WHO HAVE GONE BEFORE US.

**Don't ever think there is not a significant call on your life! God never made average, only exceptional! As you and I only have extraordinary children, so does God.**

Yet, if you're like me, your heart aches as you see the level of darkness and deception in our broken culture, and are concerned for the future our children will inherit. **It is the storms of Earth that compel us to storm Heaven!** The history of the church of Jesus Christ has been shaped by those willing to break free from the pack. These were the true world changers! Who among us will pay the ultimate price and awaken the conscience of a sleepy church? **Revival is coming! You were made for it, and it was made for you**!

Secretariat is considered by many to be the greatest thoroughbred of all time, with the rare ability for both stamina and speed. The more Secretariat ran, the faster he would get. In 1973, he won the Triple Crown, setting race records that stand today in all three events (Kentucky Derby, Preakness Stakes and the lengthy Belmont).

Secretariat was known for still accelerating as he crossed the finish line. After he died, an autopsy revealed he had been born with an enlarged heart. What a great principle! **A big heart can help us run hard, even to our last days. "Jesus, give us big hearts to follow hard after You!"**

Frank Bartleman was a journalist with a big heart. When the Azusa Street Revival broke out in Los Angeles in 1906, God used him to chronicle what He was doing and help spread the revival. **He fasted, prayed, wrote and published, using the gifts God gave him.**

At times, personal prophecies are shared with us that resonate deeply. I have received prophecies that I have a Secretariat and Frank (Francis) Bartleman anointing on my life. The three races Secretariat ran match critical needs in every city: **Unity amongst leaders, Reconciliation between races, and the stamina to run the marathon race for Revival.** The specifics of these pro-phetic words are very personal, so I will not share them here, but I bring them up to encourage us, that we are all running a race that others ran before us. Connecting these prophetic dots will help each of us finish well.

**SCRIPTURE** *"But you be watchful in all things, endure afflictions, do the work of an evangelist, fulfill your ministry." (2Timothy 4:5, NLT)*

# PLAYING HIDE AND SEEK WITH GOD

**PRINCIPLE:** GOD IS ALWAYS DRAWING US TO STEP OUT IN FAITH.

Ever play "hide and seek" when you were a child. It was fun! But it's not just for children. God wants to play "hide and seek" with you and me every day. It's the only way to live a supernatural life.

The Bible says, "It is the glory of God to conceal things, but the glory of kings is to search things out." (Proverbs 25:2, ESV) and, "You will seek me and find me. When you seek me with all your heart..." (Jeremiah 29:13, ESV) Jesus added, "Ask, and it will be given to you; seek, and you will find; knock, and it will be opened to you." (Matthew 7:7, NKJV) and even shared this same principle in a parable, "The kingdom of heaven is like treasure hidden in a field, which someone found and hid; then in his joy he goes and sells all that he has and buys that field." (Matthew 13:44, NKJV)

God's hiding, but He wants you to find Him! It will allow you to experience what is far greater than any adventure...a relationship with the living God! But this can only take place if we walk by faith in God's Word, and not by feelings.

**I've found in life the least trustworthy things I can count on are feelings, and the most trustworthy is the Bible. Faith in God's Word is the miraculous ingredient that guides me to God, and activates true joy in my life. Whereas happiness waits to see what's going to happen, joy blissfully opens its arms to every moment, choosing in advance to see life from God's point of view.**

You could describe joy as "a deep sense of inner satisfaction that comes from seeing our lives from God's perspective, and responding properly to the challenges and suffering of life." **Joy comes in the morning, before anything has happened to make us happy! We can opt to let fear or worry come in the morning, or perhaps even depression and disappointment. It's always our choice! If we so desire, we can invite discouragement for breakfast, take hopelessness out to lunch, and join despair for a candlelight dinner. It's always our call.**

**Will you choose joy today? Will you find God by faith, and stand upon His Word and promises?**

**SCRIPTURE** *"Count it all joy, my brothers, when you meet trials of various kinds, for you know that the testing of your faith produces steadfastness. And let steadfastness have its full effect, that you may be perfect and complete, lacking in nothing." (James 1:2-4)*

**PRINCIPLE:** GOD WILL SPEAK TO US IN WAYS THAT WILL BRAND OUR FUTURE STEPS.

One of my favorite experiences in life is going on retreats to fast and pray with prophetic intercessors. God always shows up in such marvelous ways. One special place we stay and spend time in corporate worship and prayer is the Home of Peace in Oakland, California, an historic site where legends of the faith have spent time seeking God. God's anointed presence is always rich there; day or night. **There is a keen sense that giants have walked the worn wood floors feeling the same inadequacy I feel, but looking to Jesus to be the difference maker. The unity of joining with trusted friends and equally desperate souls is truly invigorating.**

On one occasion, I left the group praying in the chapel, and as I walked into the men's room I was specifically pondering the question, "God, what's ahead in believing for a revival?" There in front of me, in perfect order, were eight rolls of toilet paper, precisely stacked, each roll facing me with the word, "MARATHON" in bold letters. Typically, there may be a couple of rolls, but eight...preaching at me! It was like a splash of cold water. Immediately, I received the answer to my question, and it has been life to my hungry soul.

Being a Christian is a marathon! Those who finish well have one thing in common. They remained faithful! But, since we are all at times faithless, the one Person who can keep us faithful is the only One who truly is faithful...God Himself. The Bible says, "If we are faithless, He remains faithful; He cannot deny Himself." He cannot deny who He created us to be. Our unfaithfulness can't dissolve God's faithfulness. His faithfulness continually draws us back to Him. If we'll let it, God's faithfulness is designed to even transform us. It is one of the benefits of knowing Him.

**The fruit of God's Spirit is faithfulness. What does faithfulness to God look like? I believe it's when we are committed to doing nothing without Him; then He can trust us to do His will.**

SCRIPTURE *"Therefore, since we are surrounded by so great a cloud of witnesses, let us also lay aside every weight, and sin which clings so closely, and let us run with endurance the race that is set before us, looking to Jesus, the founder and perfecter of our faith, who for the joy that was set before him endured the cross, despising the shame, and is seated at the right hand of the throne of God." (Hebrews 12:1-2)*

166. 2TIMOTHY 2:13, NKJV
167. GALATIANS 5:23

**PRINCIPLE:** THE ONLY WAY GOD CAN GROW AND GROOM US IS BY STRETCHING OUR FAITH MUSCLES.

In 2016, I ran into a friend I had not seen in 20 years. He said, "You know that booklet you wrote, 'Are You Going To Heaven? Two Question Test Reveals The Startling Answer[168]'? Well, a church in the Philippines in the mid-80's used it to birth their church, and multiplied thousands came to Jesus because of it. **Now, it is one of the largest churches in Asia with 85,000 people, and your booklet was one of the principal tools accelerating that growth.**" I was floored and, to say the least, greatly encouraged.

A month after this serendipitous testimony, I received an email from a lawyer[169] who wrote, "We met around 1992 when you spoke at my church... Fairfax Covenant Church... At the end of the sermon...you quoted I Samuel 30:19, 'But nothing of theirs was missing ... David brought it all back.' Then you said something like, 'I don't know what situation you are facing, but this verse will help guide you to the right answer on what to do.' ...your word provided guidance on what do to, and we had a fantastic outcome. Our church was renting a school for its Sunday morning meetings, and the school district was charging us (and other area churches) five times the regular rental rate because we were a church."

"Your word brought unity and...the lawsuit (we filed) has borne amazing fruit, even to this day. Our church received back the $235,000 it had paid in overcharges... Among legal scholars, the court decision from the Federal Appeals Court...is viewed as the leading (and correct) decision that school boards cannot charge community groups different rental rates to use their facilities for their meetings... **So churches have saved countless amounts of money in higher rent they never had to pay because of what you said to us that morning about 24 years ago.** Churches may be open and not closed today because of what you set off by speaking at our church that morning... thank you for your faithfulness in bringing the Word of the Lord to us...it shows that we as Christians never know how far the Lord will have our act of faithfulness reverberate for the good of many others."

It takes my breath away! **Obedient seeds always bear more fruit than we know.**

---

**SCRIPTURE** *"Plant your seed in the morning and keep busy all afternoon, for you don't know if profit will come from one activity or another—or maybe both." (Ecclesiastes 11:6, NLT)*

168. THE 'TWO QUESTION TEST' BOOKLET IS AVAILABLE AT CHRISTIAN EQUIPPERS INTERNATIONAL, WWW.EQUIPPER.COM
169. JORDAN LORENCE, SENIOR COUNSEL, ALLIANCE DEFENDING FREEDOM, WASHINGTON D.C.

# GOD'S SAVING THE BEST WINE FOR LAST

**PRINCIPLE:** BELIEVE GOD TO MOVE UPON YOUR FAMILY, CHURCH, REGION AND NATION.

A catalyst for the Protestant Reformation, Martin Luther was asked, "If Jesus was coming back tomorrow, what would you do?" He replied, "I'd plant a tree." This speaks to our need to be about our heavenly Father's business all the days of our lives. Jesus said, "Occupy till I come."

Similarly, the great evangelist D.L. Moody was asked, "If Jesus was going to come back in five minutes, what would you do?" He said, "I'd finish my steak." Moody wasn't being brash; he was making an important point. Whatever we are doing should be appropriate, and God's will, in the event Jesus comes for us, or we die and are taken to Him. Though we all fail, "living ready to face God" must be the goal for each of our lives in every moment.

**The fact is: life has not cheated us! And none of our regrets are worth dwelling on! The greatest lessons in life come from learning to respond properly to what we think is a "Failure or Loss." God alone is able to use our seeming setbacks for good—as we trust Him. Instead of sinking me, the pressures in my life actually anchor me to the One who loves me most. Whether my life's an adventure or a disaster is in my court. I choose "adventure," not because it's easy or because I know what's ahead, but because I've seen the faithfulness of the One who holds my future in His safe and loving hands.**

Do you believe God has a marvelous future for your life? I've found nothing jars me more than a left-hook from nowhere that rocks my world. So, it's important to ask, "Am I merely preparing my heart for what I consider success, or am I getting ready for the inevitable reality of learning to overcome a major setback...or severe struggle?" Jesus said, "If anyone would come after me, let him deny himself and take up his cross and follow me."

**Am I practically, tangibly, daily, preparing my heart to take up my cross... dying to myself...dying to my will, but fully alive and believing for the resurrecting power of Jesus? I accept the reality that I am dying to live, and that my future is bright because my Heavenly Father is the Author.**

---

**SCRIPTURE** *"For I am about to do something new. See, I have already begun! Do you not see it? I will make a pathway through the wilderness. I will create rivers in the dry wasteland." (Isaiah 43:19, NLT) "...I believe God that it will be just as it was told me." (Acts 27:25, NKJV) the founder and perfecter of our faith, who for the joy that was set before him endured the cross, despising the shame, and is seated at the right hand of the throne of God." (Hebrews 12:1–2)*

170. LUKE 19:13, KJV
171. MATTHEW 16:24

# EPILOGUE

What does a healthy, supernatural, Christian life look like? It will always look...unfamiliar...unexpected!

If you and I keep experiencing the same challenges and adventures, it probably means we're going in a circle. God has never duplicated a molecule or a moment. He never eats leftovers, and doesn't watch reruns. Neither should we! Those who truly follow Him can expect the unexpected.

The last week of June 2016, as I had just finished writing this daily devotional, Suzie and I moved into a rental home. Aside from professional movers hauling larger items, we moved many of our possessions ourselves over three very hot and long summer days. It was grueling, with temperatures around 106 degrees. Noticing a grumpy attitude was coming upon me, I put my iPhone in my back pocket and listened to an audio version of the Book of Job over and over again for all three days. The struggles of Job were so massive that what I was facing paled in comparison.

While listening to Job for many hours as I worked, carrying box after box, I was impacted by two particular reflections: How insensitive Job's friends were, and how God restored everything when he prayed for his friends. It reminded me of when I was a young Christ-follower. I felt the Old Testament prophets were fixated on God's judgment. As I grew in maturity and read them again, I was overwhelmed with His mercy.

The only context I had for the convicting verses in the Book of Job during those three difficult days was my own heart and attitude toward people I had known who had suffered unthinkable loss. I was convicted that my response had at times been judgmental, critical, and less than compassionate and sympathetic. I had no idea that the very next day, a series of situations would provide the backdrop for Job's experience, and a perfect storm for an emotional upheaval.

On Friday, July 1st, a number of events took place:

**PERSONAL BLESSING:** Our house closed escrow and money was deposited into our account. With a difficult real estate market in our area, Suzie and I considered this sale a divine blessing.

**KINGDOM ADVANCEMENT**: A website we had been working on for over a year — HUBlife.org (Heal Breaches, Unite Believers, and Build Bridges) — had its soft-launch.

**SPIRITUAL WARFARE:** My Gmail was hacked on July 1st, and all of my incoming and outgoing emails went to trash for a few days following.

**FAMILY ATTACK:** I received an unexpected phone call about a very serious extended family situation that was going public on that day, and would have serious repercussions on our 40 years of family unity.

These were a startling series of events ranging from blessing and favor with the sale of our house and launching of a healing website, but, likewise, personal attacks against myself and my loved ones. They affirmed that God wanted to bless my life and ministry, but also that the battle was joined and my unexpected future would have new, and even greater, challenges.

**RACIAL CONFLICTS:** Following that, I flew to Singapore for a week to speak in a church on July 5th, the same day an African-American man was shot and killed by police in Baton Rouge, Louisiana, followed on July 8th with 12 officers shot and five killed in Dallas, Texas. This began hours of emails, texts, and long-distance phone calls with Police Department and African-American leaders in the Sacramento region. All in preparation for an upcoming Sacramento Police and Community City Awards Celebration in September, primarily sponsored by Sacramento's African-American Churches.

It was a very emotional, precarious week in Singapore processing battles on many fronts: my extended family and race relations in our city and nation.

So, what am I to learn from this perfect storm? God wants to encourage us with our future, while simultaneously alerting us to its essential challenges that are divinely crafted to produce in us what an easier journey would not.

All of us would rather positive things happen to us than negative. Yet, we need both in order to become the people God created us to be. Though I enjoy pleasure more than pain, both motivate me. Though I am grateful to be going to Heaven, the possibility of rebelling and going to Hell compels me. Spoiling children can be just as damaging as being overbearing. If I am never willing to do the hard things, the painful things, even the most difficult things, I will not become the person God designed me to be. The Bible says, "If we endure hardship, we will reign with him."

Today, two roads are before each of us: the easy road and the hard road, the expected and the unexpected. Which will help you become the person you really want to be?

 The unexpected supernatural is coming and will provide each of us a huge wakeup call! It will test our true motives, which is the dimension God wants to refine in us. The Bible says, "Every man's way is right in his own eyes, but the Lord weighs and examines the hearts [of people and their motives]."[175]

"People say they love truth, but in reality they want to believe that which they love is true."[176]

In the Old Testament, the children of Israel soon forgot the miseries of Egypt, and would have exchanged the familiar slavery of their past for the uncertain freedom of their future. Like Lot's wife, we each tend to look back...even when we know there's nothing there.

C. S. Lewis, in his book Perelandra, speaks of the "love of money as the root of all evil,"[177] an "...itch to have things over again, as if life were a film that could be unrolled twice..." Was this the root of all evil, craving the false comfort of repetition, rather than the creative unknown, birthed in the heart of a safe and all-wise God?

Lewis suggests that the chief reason people love money is "...a defense against chance, a security for being able to have things over again, a means of arresting the unrolling of the film." This begs the question, is our pursuit of money and things at times an attempt to restrain our Creator from initiating something brand new and fresh in our lives? And is this done because we really don't trust Him?

How can we live a supernatural life without a fresh expectancy for all He's planned for us?

Trust the God of the unexpected! Believe all He has written in your script will work for your good and make you the person He created you to be!

Paul the Apostle's advice is so appropriate. He said, "...one thing I do: forgetting what is behind and straining toward what is ahead, I press on toward the goal to win the prize for which God has called me heavenward in Christ Jesus."[178]

Jesus, we trust You and Your marvelous plans for us. Help us to never question their value and Your ultimate intention that they will work for our good.

175. PROVERBS 21:2, AMP
176. ROBERT J. RINGER, AMERICAN ENTREPRENEUR, SPEAKER AND AUTHOR
177. 1TIMOTHY 6:10
178. PHILIPPIANS 3:13-14, NIV

# HEAVEN COMES TO EARTH

Our lives consist of moments!

They form memories, some memorable, and some forgettable!

This is a truly memorable moment in the summer of 2016, when hundreds of men from *Real Life Church*, pastored by Scott Hagan, gathered for a men's meeting. *Sacramento's Police Chief*, Sam Somers, was invited to the stage to be prayed for. What was intended to be a brief season, went on and on, with African-American men hugging him, tears streaming down their faces. It is now an iconic image of what Jesus can do to heal and unite a city when hearts are yielded to His Holy Spirit.

May it happen in your city as well.

# RECOMMENDED BOOKS

BOOKS AVAILABLE AT WWW.FRANCISANFUSO.COM

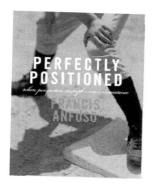

### Perfectly Positioned—When Perspective Triumphs Over Circumstance

Do you wish God had written a different script for you? Do you see your life as an exquisite feast or burnt toast? Are you eating and enjoying every bite or is it boring, bland and predictable? Are you filled with regret and shame or hope and healing? Our lives begin to be truly transformed when we stop asking God to change our circumstances, and allow Him to change our perspective! Behind every challenging situation there is a loving God whose victorious perspective is far greater than the trials we face. God's will is that we would embrace the life He has given us, instead of wishing for what does not exist and would not satisfy even if it did. If you have come to the realization that you have fished all night and caught nothing, it is not an accident. Keep fishing! God has perfectly positioned you to read this book. The breakthrough you have been longing for is just ahead!

### Living Perfectly Positioned— "Loving Life" Devotional Series

This book could be called: "The Greatest Hits of Perfectly Positioned." The best of the best revelations are in bite-size, one-a-day pieces. Instead of wishing you had a different script for your life, God can renew your mind to enjoy the only life you have. By changing your perspective, you will see your life changed! God's will is that we would embrace the life He has given us, instead of wishing for what does not exist and would not satisfy even if it did. If you have come to the realization that you have fished all night and caught nothing, it's not an accident. Keep fishing! God has perfectly positioned you to read this book. The breakthrough you have been longing for is just ahead!

### Identity / Destiny Prayer Journal

The first step in fulfilling your destiny is finding your identity, and only God knows the answer to this question. My true identity is who He created me to be. My ultimate destiny is what He has called me to do. In our natural life we will only see what we are willing to focus upon. But..."In prayer there is a connection between what God does and what you do." Matthew 6:14 (MSG) It is in prayer that God helps us understand Him in fresh ways and deeper levels. We connect with Him and He unlocks His kingdom within us. Inside this 40-Day Prayer Journal you will examine areas of life that will call for new focus and connected prayer. In so doing, you will experience the endlessly delightful relationship He promises.

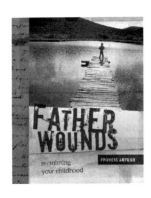

### Father Wounds—Reclaiming Your Childhood

As an abandoned and abused son, my soul suffered long-term destruction. But my wounded heart was exactly what God wanted to heal and restore. I discovered God is the Father I always wanted. He's the perfect Dad I needed all along. God can help you forgive the parent who hurt you. He wants to heal you completely and use you mightily in the lives of others! Today is the day to step into the wholeness and destiny God has for His children!

### Church Wounds—
### Francis Anfuso and David Loveless

Our wounds don't have to disable us. They're meant to be a doorway into the restored life God always intended. God wants to heal us, if we want to be. For God to free us, we must allow Him to touch our pain. Church Wounds examines the most common hurts inflicted by Christians on Christians: hypocrisy, judgmentalism, leader insensitivities, and abuse, plus many more. Read the stories of those who were not just hurt—but healed; and then experience the healing yourself.

### NUMB

We all fight numbness and its long-term effect. Unless our daily reality is greater than our inner fantasy, we'll wander from one reality-replacement to another. When we forget what we know—we forfeit who we are.

Everything God does is designed to lead us into intimacy with Him—to set us free from boredom, loneliness, and self-absorbed distractions. He loves us enough to allow us to be satisfied with only Himself.

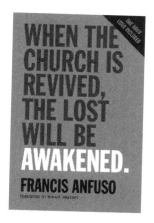

### AWAKENED

What would it take to:

- awaken a nation that has ceased to depend upon God?
- awaken the mind of those who no longer fear or reverence Him?
- awaken the conscience of those who have grown numb to discerning good and evil?
- awaken the hearts of those who consider it a choice to end the lives of their unborn children, while rejecting God's order for marriage and the family?
- revive the spirit of a church that has grown sleepy and indifferent toward the broken world around them?

What would it take? It would take a move of God... a revival of Biblical proportions! Rekindle your passion for Jesus and prepare for the sovereign outpouring we so desperately need. May we each find our unique role for all that is ahead and be fully protected during the ensuing battle.

### 2029—The Church of the Future*

You can comprehend the future if you study the past and discern the present. God is not hiding what is about to happen. He longs to reveal it to us. In 1989, Francis Anfuso wrote We've Got a Future—The 21st Century Church. Now, two decades after its release, the book reads like a detailed depiction of today's church. But the story is far from finished. This next volume details what is about to unfold—where the church must go, and the significant role you can play. 2029 is a glimpse into our future. A taste of what will shortly come to pass. Now is not the time for the Church to shrink back and recoil as the battle rages. Instead, we are approaching our finest hour.

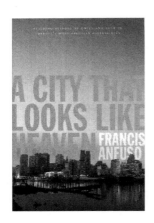

### A CITY THAT LOOKS LIKE HEAVEN

When gold was discovered in 1848 near Sacramento, thousands of eager prospectors came from all over the world to seek their fortune. Soon the easy to find gold was gone, and many found themselves destitute, sick, and penniless. Helping to care for these weary souls were a handful of Christian pastors.

In 1850, when California became a state, a decade before the Civil War, there was an attempt to make it a slave state. Once again, Sacramento pastors stood in the gap against injustice toward African-Americans and were persecuted for it. At the same time, they affirmed the rights of Chinese immigrants who were being treated unfairly.

Now, 168 years later, Time Magazine has called Sacramento: "America's Most Racially Diverse City". Once more, a great treasure is waiting to be discovered... hidden within our cultural diversity. Geologists insist 80% of California's Mother Lode gold is still in the ground, but it just costs too much to extract. The relational gold of racial harmony and church unity lies underneath our feet and begs the question: Do we know the treasure we've been given?

48086467R00093

Made in the USA
San Bernardino, CA
16 April 2017